The Power of Less

Essays on Poetry and Public Speech

To Pat Murray —
I hope there are warm
words for cold days —

Samuel Hoyt
2/4/2007

Samuel Hazo

The Power of Less

Essays on Poetry and Public Speech

MARQUETTE
UNIVERSITY

PRESS

Library of Congress Cataloging-in-Publication Data

Hazo, Samuel John.
 The power of less : essays on poetry and public speech / Samuel Hazo.
   p. cm.
 ISBN-13: 978-0-87462-013-9 (pbk. : alk. paper)
 ISBN-10: 0-87462-013-9 (pbk. : alk. paper)
 1. Poetry. I. Title.
 PN1031.H37 2005
 809.1—dc22

                                                2005024889

Samuel Hazo is the founder and director of the International Poetry Forum in Pittsburgh, Pennsylvania, and McAnulty Distinguished Professor of English Emeritus at Duquesne University, where he taught for 43 years.

Cover art by Nancy Leavitt ©2005.
Nancy Leavitt calligraphic painting of Mark Rutter's *Reading the Difficult Poet*.

Association of American
University Presses

MARQUETTE UNIVERSITY PRESS
MILWAUKEE

The Association of Jesuit University Presses

Acknowledgements

This book is dedicated to the late Dr. Joseph Schwartz, a brilliant scholar, educator, and trusted friend for many years. During his tenure as editor of *Renascence* he invited me to write essays on T.S. Eliot and Richard Wilbur, both of which are included.

I would also like to thank Anne Mullin Burnham for a close pre-reading of the essays and for a number of helpful suggestions. Special thanks are due to Melissa Altenderfer for carefully preparing the manuscript for publication.

—Samuel Hazo

Some of these essays have appeared in
Renascence,
Poets and Writers, and
The Translation Review.

Table of Contents

INTRODUCTION

From the time of the earliest cultures to the present, poets have been seen as the most reliable witnesses because they are not only veritable "seers" of the exterior and interior world, but they are able to convey their experience of it to others in language. And such expressions present us with visions of the world within and the world without that are not only particular to each poet but are also capable of being shared by us. Somehow this experience transforms our outlook and our very values in ways that nothing else can do.

The greatest poets in history have endured because their expressed visions have helped us see and feel those things that are permanently true of the human condition. In our era when so much of what passes for poetry is really sociology, ideology, rhetoric or mere wordplay, it is well to be reminded of the fact that great poetry is more—much more—than that. Whether it inspires insight or wonder, visionary poetry is more than a different use of language. It is another language—a language that always manages to outlive its authors, its circumstances and the time of its creation. Poems come into existence out of absolute and unavoidable and largely inexplicable necessity. They are ongoing presences, and ongoing presences have no past tense because they always exist in the now. In this sense, Ezra Pound noted, all literature—if it is literature at all—is contemporary.

Each of the essays in this book deals with some aspect of poetry's visionary nature—its awe-inspiring impact; its reliance upon feeling as being more dependable a form of knowledge than the conclusions of science or discursive reason; its capacity to convey the mysterious so that the final result is not mere pleasure but wisdom; its essential difference from mere verse; its challenge to translators who struggle to re-create in one language what is poetically present in another; its capability of inspiring poets to spring the locks of falsifying or stultifying forms of expression in order to say what they feel and see as they actually felt and saw it.

All of these aspects of poetry are based on a longstanding view that poetic inspiration writes the poet and not vice-versa. Poems cannot be willed into being. The true poet, as Plato and Keats believed, is the instrument by and through which a poem is realized in a moment of insight or transport. In this sense true poems are momentary epiphanies, and they are invariably as brief as they are unforgettable. They startle us into the present and keep us there as long as we are in their grip. Like kisses or tears they have no past (or future) tense. Like telegrams they eschew the superfluous and value the vital—only the vital. They emphasize the power of less. This is not simply a matter of minimum wordcount. There are complete poems, to be sure, that are only one-line long. There are others of many lines, but the lines spring from a single nucleus and have an equally singular focus throughout. The focus is what is important.

In this regard poetry stands opposed to those social forces that equate significance with "more-ness" or with what is bigger and better. It may seem like a contradiction to state that poetry is proof that, in artistic terms, less is more, but it is true. In their very succinctness poem after poem demonstrates this—no passenger words, no padding, no irrelevancies.

In life as in literature (since every crisis in literature is a crisis in life) the same principle applies and with the same undeniable force. After the catastrophe of September 11, 2001, for example, there were poems and speeches written and spoken by many who tried to capture the sheer horror and pain of that event. Occasionally a poem would succeed in whole or in part. The oratory, especially the oratory of political figures, often veered into mere declamation and overstatement by trying to say what we in our hearts knew could never really be said. That became even more obvious on the anniversary of the event in 2002 when one television network devoted one hour to comments by firefighters and policemen who had survived what had killed many of their companions. These men and women had a difficult time saying what they really felt, but each of them conveyed, both in what they said and what they left unsaid, the scope of their individual tragedy within the overall tragedy. Everyone who listened could not help but be touched and moved by their words and, above all, by the silences between the words where the real poetry existed. It made all the other public commentary and editorializing seem shallow in comparison and almost unworthy of the subject.

Ezra Pound once wrote that a poet was someone who, believing in silence, could not at times keep himself from speaking. If this is true, then poetry is akin to utterance. And utterance is more primordial than speech because it is nine-tenths involuntary—a gasp, a scream, an outburst like the "small, white cries of love" that can no longer be contained. And often the briefer the utterance, the more powerful it is. A basic principle of physics applies here, i.e., the more you reduce the volume, the more you increase the pressure. Perhaps Gustave Flaubert was really saying the same thing in different words when he claimed that "human speech is like a cracked kettle on which we tap crude rhythms for bears to dance to, while we long to make music that will melt the stars." By serving as the autobiographers of everybody, visionary poets create this music with the distinctive power of less.

Samuel Hazo

"And take upon us the mystery of things
As if we were God's spies."

—William Shakespeare
King Lear V, iii

1

TO UGLIFY OR BEAUTIFY

Poetry begins where logic stops, or rather where logic cannot go. At that point poetry obeys its own logic, which is not the same as the logic of reason. It "outs," not on concepts or conclusions, but in images. A literalist, for example, might define silence as a time that is soundless. Dylan Thomas thought of silence as a "needle passing through water."

The mother-source of the truth of poetry is the imagination, and Plato was correct to say that such truth comes to us as a gift and not as a result of our limited efforts to discover it. We cannot reason ourselves into a poem any more than we can reason ourselves into faith. Poetry and belief have this in common. They come to exist within us in their own good time and at their own preference, never at ours. We cannot summon either of them when we choose any more than we can summon the exact moment when we will experience undeniable love for a particular person. Poetry and faith and love rhyme in this way. We are unable to initiate through our own power what prompts any of the three to possess us. We can only acquiesce and cooperate with them when they do, which is why poets and saints and lovers are said to be "touched" or chosen. They are incapable of choosing themselves.

True poets always provide us with what T.S. Eliot called "a sense of the genuine." We experience a vision of life through their words and know without proof or statistics that these words are as authentic as oaths sworn before God, which, in the spiritual sense, they are. We discern it in Eliot's: "The last temptation is the greatest treason./To do the right thing for the wrong reason." Or in William Butler Yeats': "The best lack all conviction while the worst/Are filled with passionate intensity." Or in "Why We Are Truly a Nation" by William Matthews:

> Because we rage inside
> the old boundaries,
> like a young girl leaving the Church
> scared of her parents.
>
> Because we all dream of saving
> the shaggy dung-caked buffalo,
> shielding the herd with our bodies.
>
> Because grief unites us,
> like the locked antlers of moose
> who die on their knees in pairs.

It is this visionary character of poetry that makes it essential to any life that presumes to be called human. Without it we are doomed to "live through" our days as so many disconnected episodes until we are finally buried by history. Visionary poetry enables us to transcend our fate en route——"to see life steadily," in Matthew Arnold's words, "and to see it whole." Poets who possess this visionary gift (it is more than mere skill) see beneath the facts to the hidden truth and in their poetry permit us to see it as well. Most of them would be hesitant to call themselves poets in the same way that genuine Christians rarely identify themselves as such. Better, they believe, to continue the chosen servitude of trying to qualify rather than to proclaim such qualification in advance or at all. Chaucer's "The life so short, the craft so long to learn" would probably strike them as every writer's best guideline as well as the most humbling. The rest—to borrow from Ecclesiastes—is vanity.

How can society accommodate such visionaries? Among the dogmatic majority who spend their lives convinced that they are right while the rest of mankind is wrong, visionary poets are often regarded as fools. After all, a poet cannot prove the truth of his utterances by logic or science or in any other way. He can only profess, like any good witness, that he has simply expressed what he has seen or sensed, albeit through the prism of his own temperament and perspective. His only credential is concern. Like Cassandra he is often blessed with a true insight into what is happening in the present moment, but he is also cursed with the fact that no one really cares at all about what he sees or says, which is often worse than outright denial. Before the outbreak of World War II Bertolt Brecht wrote: "The common people know that war is coming. When the leaders talk peace, the mobilization orders have already been signed." Brecht's prescience was greeted with indifference. And the war came.

If poets are—in Shelley's words—the world's "unacknowledged legislators," then our need for poetry is not optional. We need it daily in the same way that we need air. One poet has even gone so far as to say that poetry is "the voice that is great within us." The important word is us. To those who say that poetry is peripheral to human life and thus dispensable, we can only respond by conjuring up for their edification the sterility of their implied alternative: a world of unrelieved work that inevitably degenerates into mere toil, a world where the imagination atrophies in the name of political purity until society turns into a cultural gulag or wasteland, a world that becomes not only less beautiful but gradually and willfully uglier, a world that becomes the exact opposite of what God intended us to make of it.

If poetry is peripheral and not essential, as some of its detractors insist, why is it that those who seek to impose totalitarian or "politically correct" strictures upon their societies immediately single out poets as enemies of the state and mark them for ridicule, exile or death? The answer is obvious. Poets are those who cannot excuse themselves from expressing what is actually happening in and at the moment. As such they are the natural enemies of all those who would bend others to their manipulative will because they regard people as sheep or simply as multitudes governable only by deception, lies or brute fear. Poetry, on the contrary, introduces awe into our lives, and awe is the beginning of the wonder of wisdom, and wisdom inevitably returns us to our own humanity. And whatever returns us to our humanity makes us the opponents of those who are not beautifiers but uglifiers who want to take the wonder out of our lives, whose goal is not to enlighten but to dominate. Adrian Mitchell once defined a poet as "someone who comes to terms with his own amazement." To be amazed and to amaze others by writing or saying so... not a bad credential by any standard.

2

FEAR OF FEELING

The expression of precise emotion is much more difficult than the expression of precise thought. Anyone who has ever attempted to translate feelings into words, whether orally or in writing, knows how daunting such a translation can be. At times we fail completely. At other times we wait until the emotion ebbs and then speak of it (rather than speak it) safely in the past tense. We tell ourselves reassuringly that this is what civilized people do. They wait until they can speak "rationally," until the mood passes, until they can say something in the dispassionate tones of the passive voice.

Our predilection for waiting for feelings to cool before they can be considered worthy of expression is all too common in the *post facto* mood of much of our public life. We delay until it's "safe" to speak, which means that we wait until we have nothing of interest or consequence to say about something that once moved us deeply. According to this mode of behavior we would not express our feelings for Roxane in the words of Rostand's Cyrano: "I love you, I'm overwhelmed, I love you to the point of madness! Your name is in my heart like a bell shaken by constant trembling, ringing day and night: Roxane, Roxane, Roxane. Loving everything about you, I forget nothing." We would rather wait and then say: "Roxane, you are loved by me."

People who defend such retreats from true expression do so on the assumption that the reasonable is preferable to the emotional. Not only preferable but somehow more trustworthy. Such an assumption immediately separates thought from feeling although, in our very daily lives and in our very natures, no such separation exists. Nor is such a separation desirable without our doing injury to our very ways of apprehending the world and one another.

Thought and feeling interpenetrate one another constantly, and this is as it should be. The aspiring total rationalists among us are constantly fighting a rear-guard action with emotional reality, and sentimentalists eventually wake up to the fact that they do have minds. Too few practice what Fernando Pessoa preached: "Most people think with their feelings, whereas I feel with my thinking." Eventually it becomes a matter of achieving daily and even hourly the true marriage of feeling and thought. If we over-trust one at the expense of the other, writers like Julian Barnes are there to remind us that we must finally realize that we are dealing not so much with a problem as with a mystery. Which is why Barnes may have been prompted to write with his customary but welcome cynicism: "I am sentimental about clarity of thought, emotional about rationality."

When we are moved to express ourselves, the secret is to realize that we do not tap our deeper natures until we utter "felt thoughts" and find ways to put what Jacques Maritain called "intelligenciated sense" into words.

In this regard it is enlightening to think of instances that occur and reoccur when the expression of "felt thoughts" is demanded or expected of us: in the expression of gratitude, in proposing toasts, in extending our condolences, in venting our spleen. As an example of thanks well said, there is an illustrative episode in the later life of Jan Sibelius. Marian Anderson had gone to Helsinki to appear in a concert celebrating Sibelius' ninetieth birthday. It so happened that Sibelius was unable to attend the concert because the weather kept him housebound. On the day following the celebration, Marian Anderson traveled to his home and gave the entire concert for Sibelius alone. When she finished, the old man rose, made his way to her, took her hand and kissed it and said, "Miss Anderson, the roof of my house is too low for you." In the genre of toasts, it is difficult to find anything to top Winston Churchill's tribute to the RAF for turning the tide in the Battle of Britain: "Never has so much been owed by so many to so few." And when it comes to the expression of condolence, I can think of nothing in recent history to match Georges Pompidou's succinct announcement to the nation of the death of Charles de Gaulle: "Tonight France is a widow." And since anger and rage definitively involve our emotions, it is edifying to compare the rather limited vocabulary of the seemingly virile among us (in which the word for mating is used—usually in error—as a verb, adjective, adverb and interjection) with the following ingenious curse from the pen of the French poet Robert Desnos: "Cursed be the father of the bride of the blacksmith who forged the iron for the axe with which the oak was felled from which the bed was carved in which was conceived the great grandfather of the man who was driving the carriage in which your mother met your father."

There is no question that the language of "felt thought" must be quarried from our personal depths. Like the best gold it does not lie on the surface. One of the diseases of much public discourse today is that it has become so much disembodied prattle. The "talk shows" are not showcases for talk but naked blab in which any blabbermouth with a microphone can and does say whatever occurs to him. Disputation is reduced to backbiting. Words tend to become disassociated from their meanings or are so sanitized into the diction of neutered non-speech (politically correct rubbish) that they end by meaning nothing at all.

The ultimate casualty at a time of the degeneration of language—in which the expression of both precise thought and precise feeling is not even regarded as necessary—is public discourse itself. Diogenes would say that the currency of social life at such a time has been debased. Take much of what passes for political debate, for example.

Of course, we all know that genuine political oratory, like acoustical music, has been adulterated by electronic enhancement. Thus speech-making is no longer an art but a technique in which public men and women are often little more than mouths for speech writers. In short, they "mouth" instead of speak. They do not feel the words at all. Often in compensation some mouthers think that making a point forcefully requires them to raise their voices, as if mere volume signifies emphasis and conviction. They apparently have never learned that lowering one's voice frequently strengthens one's argument. And any actor could tell them that nothing is louder than a whisper.

Then there is the all too common descent into lugubriousness. Nixon's tearful speech about his dog in the early nineteen fifties is a classic example, and Senator Dole's doleful farewell to the departed Nixon at the burial site in Yorba Linda is another. In both instances we were confronted with what seemed to be willed grief, which is a far cry from what one poet called the "slow snow of male tears."

The general fault with the public utterances of many political leaders is that they seem to be somehow detached from what they are saying. This makes them seem vacuous even when they are discussing serious subjects. They begin to sound like men who have never in their lives faced the possibility of sudden extinction or injury, never been brushed by tragedy's wing, never known the transforming seriousness that makes us thereafter weigh our words. On the contrary, theirs seems to be the diction of the disembodied mind. To the disembodied mind, words come as easily as easy money, and, like easy money, are spent with as little compunction and restraint as possible.

Such ultra-fluency is not the exclusive property of some politicians. There are newscasters on television and radio who have similar propensities, who "mouth" instead of speak. Since the pecking order in the broadcasting of news is to begin with the worst and proceed through a decrescendo of lesser catastrophes, one cannot help but wonder how any announcer can deliver himself of such a litany of grief on a daily basis. I've noticed that male broadcasters often "read" the news of such misfortunes with what is called professional passivity. On the other hand, many of the women seem to do so "feelingly," as if the gravity or pain of what they are describing is having or has had an effect on them. This shows at the very least that reading the news and feeling what the words are saying is, after all, possible. Dispassionate reportage or "anchorage" may be what the networks want, but I would presume that describing a tragedy like the devastation in Sarajevo or the bombing of the Murrah Building in Oklahoma would be by nature different in tone from tame announcements about a change in air fares.

Another instance of a flight from feeling surfaces in the tone of much professional criticism of either films, plays, books or music. Too often it seems to be a habit among such writers to appear to be "above" what they are considering—as if letting themselves become involved in the work from within would somehow deprive them of the objectivity needed to criticize. They seem to resist letting themselves be touched emotionally. Such a fear of feeling does a basic injustice to the work being considered because it prevents it from being experienced. The result is that the critic focuses on technique and tangential matters that are "manageable." Such critics suffer from spiritual anemia; they do not possess what every genuine critic must have—largeness of soul.

But let us return to the central matter of the expression of feeling. If all that we know comes to us through our senses (including our sixth or intuitional sense), then it is simply regrettable that we do not speak or write in ways that express this knowledge. Such habits of expression strike me as being closest to life, and at their best they are so transparent that the life shines through. But speaking in generalizations or abstractions succeeds in nothing but taking us further and further away from what it is that animates us, further and further away from those sense-created feelings that are our most reliable ways of knowing.

The most important word to stress in Eliot's statement about the greater difficulty in expressing precise emotion as opposed to precise thought is the adjective—precise. We all know how gratifying it is to say or to hear a phrase or a sentence that captures exactly an otherwise nebulous feeling. The accuracy of it leaves us pacified, gratified, satisfied.

It seems to be the nature of feelings that they move inexorably toward expression. If they do not release themselves in precise language, they can do so in guffaws, unexpected outbursts or even violence. I have often wondered if our love affair with sports and spectacles is proportionate to the outlet they provide for a lot of stored-up feelings we cannot otherwise express. Cathartic as that is, it is assuredly no substitute for the precise expression of amorphous feelings. No one would claim that a Bronx cheer or a huzzah after a touchdown is on a par with a poem of Shakespeare or Robert Frost. Ovations and applause may carry us through a weekend of overtime victories, but on Monday mornings the deeper emotional scrimmages still await us. And it is often at such times that the words of genuine poets who have preceded us or are still among us offer us the solidarity of feeling that we crave, confirming by their words our very right to feel what we feel. This confraternity of feeling over centuries and hemispheres is one of the few things that unites us as human beings—not governments, not laws, not the temporary cohesion created by national crusades, not communal gatherings against disasters like flood, earthquake or famine.

Yet among poets, especially in the past fifty years, there has been a lamentable shying away from the expression of feeling. Granted, there have been numerous poets who have literally "spilled their guts" on the page, but there is a world of difference between the expression of private as opposed to personal feelings. Personal feelings involve all of us whereas private feelings are limited to the person who is expressing them. But apart from this, there is a wealth of published poetry today that numerous critics have justifiably called hermetic. It is endemic among poets who write only for one another. They suffer from a pathetic lack of vision. Many of them are adept at the crafts of prosody, but poetry has never been equatable with mere craft. It has never been a retreat into phrase. True poetry transcends craft as it transcends individual personality. When we read or hear inspired lines, we are mysteriously put in touch with our very souls. We experience what Frost called a "stay against the flux of the world."

Shallow versifying—prosody instead of poetry, or poetry of shallow feeling or no feelings at all—does not satisfy our hunger for universal feelings precisely expressed. No wonder that students and older readers find that much poetry today does not speak to them when they are confronted by anemic examples of the genre in journals that mistake obscurantism for mystery.

Then there is the whole body of public utterance that aspires to be poetry but is nothing but heightened rhetoric. This is not precise feeling precisely expressed; rather it is plain prose overcoated with what Wordsworth would have called emotion. The most recent national example of this was Maya Angelou's recitation at the first Clinton inaugural. Forget for a moment that Maya Angelou has a wonderful sense of presence. Forget that she has a memorable face and an actress's ability to project. What she recited, despite all the panegyrics it garnered afterward, was simply not a poem. It was a litany of Americana with every ethnic "i" dotted and every 't' crossed. Its length was determined by the principle of addition and not the indispensable essence of organic form. It was not imagined as much as it was arranged. Of course, such is the fate of much "poetry" that is written for "the occasion." Invariably it fails simply because true poetry cannot be summoned on command. Norman Corwin tried it when he wrote "On a Note of Triumph" at the end of World War II. Robert Frost tried it when he wrote a poem for Kennedy's inaugural—a poem that the glinting sunlight mercifully prevented him from reading so that he had to recite "The Gift Outright" as an alternative. With Corwin and with Frost the response of poetry to a direct order was total disobedience.

Poetry has other social opponents as well. For years now we have heard advocates persuading us that we are moving inexorably toward an information-culture, whatever that means. I suspect the assumption is that information will somehow make us free.

This is asking a lot of mere information. All that information can do by its very nature is inform. It is the beginning of knowledge.

And knowledge has a long way to go before it matures into what we like to think is wisdom. But the expression of precise feeling is instantaneously transformative. It does not wait for us to digest it. It digests us. It is the ultimate change of pace that re-introduces us to what matters and what does not. Pindar was right when he gave the language of feeling its ultimate compliment: "Change the rhythm, and the walls of the city will shake."

3

Political Correctness versus Poetry

One of the biggest frauds that has become the norm in American public life at present is the myth of political correctness. Being politically correct means nothing more than saying or writing—for reasons of nicety, enforced custom or pressure—whatever is considered socially safe and usually innocuous. Thus, the purpose of the spoken or written word is no longer the search for truth but expressing what some pontificating "others" expect to hear. In other words, it's the language of servile accommodation for the sake of getting along. A more accurate definition of phoniness I cannot imagine.

Political correctness stunts and even nullifies conversation. If inoffensiveness and not candor is the social norm, how can people possibly exchange views? If any form of controversy is regarded as the equivalent of trouble-making or rudeness (and all conversations are to some extent controversial), there is no way that anyone can take issue with anything. Uniformity of thought is the ultimate consequence, and the spectacle of everyone thinking exactly alike is usually the first symptom of social slavery and degeneracy. On a deeper level, since breath is synonymous with life itself and since our words are made of breath, wasting one's breath on being politically correct is simply to waste one's life.

The predecessor of political correctness was euphemism—sweet-sounding evasions of more accurate parts of speech—rest room for toilet, funeral director for mortician or undertaker, terminated for fired, topless and bottomless for the naked body. Political correctness made euphemism a clever way of diverting attention from thorny social issues through the use of public-relations techniques and the covert devices of propaganda. Take William Safire's mintage of the word "community" as an inoffensive way of grouping blocs or tribes, i.e., the pacifist community, the sado-masochistic community, the Cuban-American community, ad nauseam. Safire is linguist enough to know that community is not the same as commonality, but so what? Community had a civilizing sound to it, and the public swallowed it without a hiccup, believing that such communities existed when in fact they did not.

You find the same euphemistic trickery afoot whenever issues involving race or gender arise. The motive behind all these circumlocutions is not to ruffle certain feathers. This is rarely called by its right name—schmoozing—but that's all it is. Its purpose is to stroke and not offend, but it really ignores the fact that certain individuals or groups make it their primary purpose in life to wait to be offended so that they can react and appear significant. The politically correct play into the hands of such people by accommodating their peevish need for public attention.

Being politically incorrect is never without its risks since it means opposing the views of the politically correct, which in most cases reflect the values of the ruling class. To oppose the Vietnam War at one time, for example, was to risk being called a traitor or a coward. Taking issue with volatile issues posed by the National Rifle Association or national policies regarding capital punishment, Cuba or the Middle East is often to invite, not debate on what are clearly debatable issues, but ridicule, blacklisting or worse. Oddly, the very ones who extol the plain fact of diversity in our country are the same people who oppose intellectual diversity on issues to which they are singlemindedly committed. Yet who would deny that intellectual diversity (as opposed to the uniformity of thought I mentioned earlier) is a much more significant sign of social progress than the often mindless blood-ties of mere ethnicity?

To change the character of public speech so that it suits the occasion or some segment of the public is to make language answerable to external rather than internal standards. And these standards invariably change with the times. The result is that political correctness is regarded as being more important than being ethically correct, historically correct, philosophically correct, grammatically correct or even democratically correct. The Presidential election of 2000 is a case in point. Despite the politically correct praises that were heaped on the strength of our democracy to survive such a contentious struggle, the fact of the matter, as everyone knows, is that the election was not decided by the halted and still and perhaps forever subjunctive popular vote count in Florida but by a single vote in Washington, D.C. And the caster of that tie-breaking vote in the Supreme Court (let's say it was Justice Scalia since he authored the majority opinion and had clearly revealed his inclination when the case was first submitted) was after all not elected nor an elector but a judicial appointee. Justice Breyer's dissent that called the verdict "a self-inflicted wound—a wound that may harm not just the Court, but the Nation" was seen by some as the politically incorrect view of another "sore loser."

It is no wonder that the politically correct have little patience with serious writers and poets. To write of things as they are, like the annoying habit of Socrates to ask why, why, why, is to disturb the complacency of the easily schmoozed as well as those who do the schmoozing. Dictators deal lethally with such writers since dictators have the nasty habit of destroying what they cannot dominate. In much of our current public prose the dispassionate is often eclipsed by the ideologically pure. The higher journalism of Walter Lippmann, James Reston, Dorothy Thompson, Theodore White, and Georgie Anne Geyer has been superceded by the slanted pedantry of the aforementioned Safire, George F. Will, and Charles Krauthammer and the equally slanted punditry of Rush Limbaugh, Oliver North, and G. Gordon Liddy.

True poetry is by nature beyond both ideology and the hypocrisy of political correctness. It reveals the permanent in what is passing. It focuses on the essential and not the superficial. The contemporary poet Philip Booth, for example, once alluded to sub-divisions as having "desert-dusty streets with fertile names" where "cheap people in expensive cars patrol the Sunday roads." Robert Lowell observed the traffic in Boston and concluded one of his best poems by writing: "a savage servility slides by on grease." Even the poetry of proverbs is visionary—"The rooster may crow, but the hen delivers"—"Poverty unites; prosperity divides"—"Men look; women notice"—"Absence will make a strong passion stronger, and a weak one weaker."

The conclusion I draw from these few examples when compared with the vacuousness of political correctness is that all of us, as users of words, are faced with a choice. Will our language be significant or mere fluff? If we want to sound like people in a void or trance, we'll be politically correct. If we'd rather experience "the inevitable solace that right language brings," there is no better means of expression than poetry. To discover what that means, read a poem. Then read it again.

4

Whatness versus Muchness

The basic difference between the poetic and the scientific view of life is that the poetic is concerned with quality, the scientific with quantity. The etymological root of quality is from the Latin *qual* (what) or *qualitas* (whatness). Quality is, therefore, irreducible, indivisible, unrepeatable and unduplicatable. It goes beyond genus and difference and other defining quantifications; it's what makes every thing itself and no other. The etymological root of quantity is *quantus* (how great or how much) or *quantitas* (greatness or muchness). The quantitative vision of reality is concerned with aspects that can be weighed, measured or otherwise identified. Philosophically speaking, these are accidents while quality is equated with essences.

By placing the poetic and the scientific attitudes at such opposite extremes (whatness versus muchness), I do not mean to suggest that scientists as a group are insensitive to quality. Loren Eiseley, himself one of the most humane and poetic of scientists, explained the difference between scientific mystery and method as follows: "In the end, science as we know it has two basic types of practitioners. One is the educated man who still has a controlled sense of wonder before the universal mystery, whether it hides in a snail's eye or within the light that impinges on that delicate organ. The second kind of observer is the extreme reductionist who is so busy stripping things apart that the tremendous mystery is reduced to a trifle, to intangibles not worth troubling one's head about."

Based on Eiseley's distinctions, I suppose that the ultimate reductionist would reduce man himself to measurable matter—a dollar's worth of chemicals or, allowing for inflation, two dollars. To the ultimate reductionist in economics man is merely a consumer. To reductionist-sociologists man might emerge as an average created by a statistical consensus. And so on.

Such reductionism unfortunately often creates a language that does not illuminate reality but distorts it. Who, for example, belongs to an average family of two-and-a-half people? No one. Who regards children as so many consumers, so many mouths to feed and no more than that? No one. This is why we do not go to reductionists for a vision of existence that touches us as human beings. We go to writers of quality—to serious writers—for that. They speak for man not in this or that aspect of his life but for all of him. And their words touch us because they confront us feelingly with our own autobiographies and not with abstractions or partialities. Eduardo Galeano emphasized this when he wrote recently: "Why does one write if not to put one's pieces together? From the moment we enter school or church, education chops us into pieces; it teaches us to divorce soul from body and mind from heart. The fishermen of the Colombian coast must be learned doctors of ethics and morality, for they invented the word *sentipensante*, feeling/thinking, to define language that speaks the truth."

If the language of poetry is essentially the language of "feeling/thinking, " then the language of science at its best is the language of substantiated accuracy concisely expressed. It seeks to bring the world we sense to measure. Its natural enemy is what cannot be proved. The scientific attitude demands at a minimum that truth must be verifiable before it can be accepted as such. If not verifiable, it is often relegated to the realm of the probable, the subjunctive, the doubtful. Poetic knowledge, on the contrary, is for the most part intuitive. Derived by its very nature from inspiration or insight, it is manifestly beyond proof. A poem strikes us as true not because it can be proved to be true (as a hypothesis can be, for example) but because its truth cannot be denied, proof or no proof. It compels our assent to its truth simply by being what it is, and we accept it, however grudgingly, because we must.

Since our society is one that seems to require endless justifications and rationales to explain our daily experiences to ourselves in conclusive terms, it is not surprising that poetry occupies a peripheral place in our cultural life. It affirms the existence of mystery in life, and mystery and conclusiveness are rarely on speaking terms. Thus the sciences and social sciences have gradually become the repositories of those aspirations and impulses that formerly led human beings to poetry or religion or mythology in search of illumination. The position that psychiatry has assumed today in this regard is a typical case in point. Without casting aspersions on the ability of certain psychologists and psychiatrists to help disturbed or disoriented people, I cannot help but conclude that they have assumed an importance beyond their limitations as behavioral scientists. Some students and numerous adults have come to regard psychiatry, for example, as the religion of our century. It offers the "answers," they claim, to the multiple dilemmas of human experience. Explanatory words like "paranoia" and "schizophrenia" and "manic depressive" are sprinkled into their conversations like pepper and salt. Human beings no longer meet but "encounter" one another. They "interface" and "interact" and "dialogue" with one another. They yearn for "meaningful relationships." Instead of thinking, they "brainstorm." Instead of discussing, they "bounce" ideas off one another. From time to time they return from "ego trips."

It may be unfair to attribute all of this argot to psychology and other related social sciences and their progeny, but there is some connection. Apart from the fact that I find such language juiceless and colorless (imagine what Romeo's "meaningful relationship" with Juliet would have sounded like if Shakespeare had expressed himself in this way or how Montaigne would have reacted to a "bounced idea"), I find it also disingenuous. It leads away from reality, not to it. This is particularly true with the language of psychiatry. So-and-so hallucinates. So-and-so has delusions of grandeur. Such descriptions are but a delineation of symptoms, and since symptoms are perceptible, they become the legitimate object of scientific inquiry within the discipline known as psychiatry. But the fruit of such inquiry is far from being an absolute. Hans Küng warned of this in *Freud and the Problem of God*: "The competence of psychoanalysis remains restricted to the field of psychological reality ... It can eliminate psychosomatic illnesses, but it cannot answer ultimate questions about meaning and meaninglessness, life and death." Regardless, seriously confused people continue to place almost blind faith in "analysis," paying high hourly sums for the attention they perhaps can no longer expect from harried or shallow friends in the belief that "analysis" all by itself will cure them. They ignore the fact that analysis etymologically means to break down into component parts. It works with ticking inanimate things like clocks. (Several years ago one of my colleagues at the university entered my office and said, "Let's talk. I want to learn what makes you tick." A teacher of psychology and a practicing psychiatrist, he assumed I would be happy to cooperate. Since I had then and still have a long-standing conviction that ticking and thinking are not synonymous and since I consider the latter nobody's business but my own, I waited until he tired of my loud silence and left). Applying analytical methods to living things, as Wordsworth noted when he wrote, "We murder to dissect," often means that the subject dies during the course of consideration—the soul of the subject, that is. Consider a tulip, for example. Growing from its sustaining bulb, it flowers upward in accordance with the organic laws of its botanical nature. Take that tulip apart and arrange its petals, its stem, its stamen and its leaves on a table, and somewhere in the process you've lost the tulip. You have all the parts, but you've lost the living flower. The whole may be the sum of its parts in the inanimate world, but the same principle does not apply in the animate.

If reductionism in psychiatry can beguile us with fractional and, to me at least, faulty views of human nature, reductionism of the same character when applied to the prosecution of criminals often makes morality irrelevant. I say this knowing that innocence does not exist in law, only non-guilt, and that legality and morality are not necessarily synonymous. But has there not been a movement in our time, largely motivated by psychological considerations, to dilute personal responsibility in criminal matters by making guilt collective or communal or attributable entirely to social or traumatic experiences that tend to absolve individuals of all accountability or blame? How many times have accused criminals been remanded to psychiatrists like so many heretics delivered to the inquisitors in order to determine their sanity or their insanity, temporary or otherwise? Robert Travers, the author of *Anatomy of a Murder*, once told me with a smirk that in Ishpemming, Michigan, where he was a sitting judge, the underground scuttlebutt had it that would-be murderers were well advised to kill six or seven at a time, never a single victim, as a sure way of qualifying for the absolution of "temporary insanity." In a more serious vein Thomas Szasz, himself a psychotherapist and the author of *The Myth of Psychotherapy*, addressed himself to the same subject in less ambiguous terms: "I submit that the courtroom psychiatrist who seeks to exonerate a killer of responsibility for his act is, from a moral point of view, an accomplice to the act of taking an innocent life .... Psychiatrists who aid and abet the insanity defense are no more inept than their accomplices are insane. Instead of calling such acts inept or insane, we ought to call them wicked and immoral."

Admittedly akin to Travers and Szasz, I believe that whatever draws us away from our core of conscience is dangerous and dehumanizing. It leads us from and not to the realities of good and evil where choices are necessary. To the extent that any psychologist, psychiatrist or any social scientist or scientists distract us from the responsibility that such choices impose upon us as individuals, to that extent, in my view, does he become less human and his largely quantitative conclusions incomplete. Accordingly, to the extent that social or physical scientists assume that a purely scientific view of man is all inclusive, to that extent do they leave out for me what is the true end of all disquisitions, namely the human spirit in all its contradictions. And I would apply this axiom to technology as well since technology is but science in its practical applications. I would include everything here from the first uses of fire to computer chips and robotics. I do not deny their value to man as aids. I only mean to suggest the level of one's human progress (or of a nation's human progress) is not synonymous with technological progress. Technology, like science, its progenitor, does not deal well with what cannot be measured or boxed into a hypothesis. Mysteries are an enigma to technology and science, but any mature human being knows that the most central of most of life's problems and questions are fraught with mystery.

In no area of human life does mystery manifest itself more enigmatically than in matters of evil, love or belief. When Edgar Allan Poe implies that the murderer in "The Black Cat" was motivated by nothing more than an "impulse to the perverse," I for one believe him. Those who prefer more scientific explanations often come up dry when attempting to explain the motives for otherwise inexplicable murders. Must an evil act always have a rational basis? Can it? Indeed, if evil is a mystery, isn't Poe's theory of an "impulse to the perverse" as convincing an explanation as any of human actions that otherwise stultify us? In matters of love, ask any person why—precisely why—he or she loves another person, and the answer will be silence or a series of probings into the inexpressible. The fact that people can find no equivalent in language for what they feel does not invalidate the feeling; it merely proves that some things cannot be said or, at any rate, said completely. If love were merely quantitative, expression would be no problem. Someone would say he loves another because she is of a certain weight, a certain height, is possessed of a specific color of hair or eye and so forth. But genuine love does not answer to such measurables. Similarly, despite the theories of those to whom mystery is anathema, love seems to be more than glandular. I was particularly heartened some time ago when Archibald MacLeish wrote that a poet can say something lasting about love only when he looks into his heart and not into his pants. And with regard to matters of belief, I was impressed when I heard Octavio Paz allude to the fact that a good many Americans are given to putting their faith into "inferior forms of credulity." I suppose he was alluding to everything from blind faith in scientology and astrology to the presumed magic of a rabbit's foot—all of the gods that cannot save.

But my reservations about the limitations of science and social science in dealing with eternal verities are not total. I confess to a deep admiration for the writings of Jung because they lead back to and not away from man. And I still think that Freud's definition of marriage as a group of two" is hard to top. Statements like these strike me as a humanly fascinating and true, and they are truthfully fascinating because the aim is to elucidate human experience and not to dehumanize it with a jargon whose specific purpose is to create the impression that man as a person is irrelevant to the explanation or solution of problems that in fact originate with him.

Lest we think that the white flashes over Hiroshima and Nagasaki were but isolated examples of technology as an all-purpose solution, we have only to consider its recent resurrection in what has come to be known as the first Gulf War. Once the war began, the vocabulary of peace and creative diplomacy became redundant. The lexicon of war took over completely. We did not have marines and infantry-men in a particular locale; we had assets. Iraq and Kuwait no longer existed as nations but as "target-rich environments." Civilian deaths were translated euphemistically into "collateral damage." And then, of course, there were "friendly casualties." A commanding general, when asked what our strategy for winning the war was, responded, "We are going to surround it (The Republican Guard), and then we are going to kill it." As necessary as this language must be for military planners, it serves technology totally by converting everything into the neuter gender. Men and women, friendly or otherwise, become so many "its" for battlefield purposes. Only later do human values reassert themselves when survivors or their kin speak after the dead and wounded are returned to their families. Victory, especially quick and carefully censored victory, may confirm the military in its use of technological jargon because many Americans believe that what works and especially what works quickly silences all opposition or amendment. And yet what would they do when confronted with the remark of one survivor of the Scud attack in Dahran twenty-four hours before the cease-fire? He said, "It blew away half my butt. Just one more day, that's all. I had a good life ahead of me." That quiet human voice somehow outspeaks and will outlive the neutered vocabularies of certain military spokesmen. Why? Because it is human. It is the same voice that A.E. Houseman made his own when he wrote in the name of the slain more that fifty years ago:

> Here dead lie we because we did not choose
> to live and shame the land from which we sprung.
> Life, to be sure, is nothing much to lose,
> but young men think it is, and we were young.

Although I would like not to think so, I suppose that the military counterpart of dehumanization and quantification might exist in the medical profession as well. The transformation of person into patient is only a step away from patient into case. I have heard such a transformation defended by some who claim that this makes objective treatment possible. Perhaps. But every time I hear such a defense I think of a story narrated by Dr. Richard Selzer in a book of his entitled *Mortal Lessons*. It so happened that one of Selzer's patients, a young wife, had a malignant tumor in her cheek. Selzer told her that the tumor had to be excised immediately, but, since it had grown around the nerve and muscle endings that supported her mouth, one side of her mouth would droop permanently after surgery. A week or so after the surgery, the young woman returned to his office to have the stitches removed from the incision. Her husband waited in the outer office. When Selzer removed the bandage, the results of the operation were evident. The woman's mouth drooped to one side. The time came when the husband was asked to come into the office. The woman, wondering whether her husband would still love her in this condition, mustered her courage and waited. The husband approached her, studied her face for a moment and then said, "It's kind of cute." Then he went to her and kissed her just to prove their kiss still worked. Selzer, observing the scene, writes that he just sat back and let all the wonder in.

For me this is not only an example of a husband's love but of medical practice in the best sense, but it also corroborates a theory attributed to Henri Bergson, namely, that science and the intuitive and mysterious cannot explain one another, that science cannot quantify quality, that mysteries cannot be reduced to measurable proportions. If love is measured by tangible considerations alone, then love would have changed in the aforementioned story as soon as the husband saw his wife's permanently changed face. Yet the very opposite happened, which proves that the measurable was not the ultimate consideration. In fact, it became almost totally irrelevant.

When a scientific outlook and an intuitive outlook find their expression in words, the results are predictably different. This difference is in fact traceable to the very difference between the scientific and the intuitive. If the truth of the language of science is measured by how accurately it accounts for the tangible world as given, then the truth of the intuitive or poetic is measured (if this is the right word) by how feelingly we express our response to the given world. The scientist's view seems to end with the facts; the poet's begins with them. A scientist might say, for example, "My mother weighs one hundred and ten pounds." And this is accurate as far as it goes. But a Chinese poet, expressing a comparable reality through the prism of his own personality and love, said, "I ran home and lifted my mother and was almost crushed by that small weight." Both men are talking about their respective mothers, but the second one, through the mystery of a poetic response, is talking about every man's mother.

The ineluctable conclusion that can be drawn from this difference in outlook and expression is that the scientist strives to state his perceptions directly, the poet indirectly. Scientific truth avoids the ambiguous or the obscure or the mysterious. The table of elements in chemistry, for example, is not an obscure listing. The poet speaks indirectly not in a spirit of circumlocution or vagueness for vagueness' sake, but because the subject he perceives does not permit itself to be expressed directly or., in some cases, at all. Hence, his reliance upon similitude. How does one write of mysteries like love or solitude or the smarting of injustice except by wrestling with the ineffable, by expressing what you are just now understanding in terms of what you already know—by saying one thing in terms of something else, by relying on metaphor, by comparing one thing to another. Metaphor is thus the key to poetry as it is the key to all forms of artistic expression. In acting, for example we are not persuaded of the validity of the portrayal until the actor (in the mystery of his craft) actually becomes the character he is portraying. Up until he reaches that point he is simply an identifiable actor as Julius Caesar or Hamlet or Willie Loman. But once he *becomes* Caesar or Hamlet or Willie Loman, once the *as* is eliminated, we are irresistibly drawn into the life that is being re-created before our eyes. We no longer have to suspend disbelief, willingly or unwillingly. This is done for us by the art of the actor. The same can be said of many of the other arts, and it is particularly true of poetry. The entire basis for poetry is metaphorical. A disappointed lover would never think that his feelings were totally expressed if he simply said that his lover disappointed him. The depth of his disappointment is somehow not equatable with a simple declarative sentence. But in William Butler Yeats' poem "The Deep-Sworn Vow" the pain of disappointment and the inability to forget are overwhelming, and they are made even more so by Yeats' restraint:

> Others because you did not keep
> That deep-sworn vow have been friends of mine.
> Yet always when I look death in the face,
> When I clamber to the heights of sleep
> Or when I grow excited with wine,
> Suddenly I meet your face.

To say that the scientific and the poetic are opposed as ways of comprehending reality is true only to the extent that they are different. But differences like these also render them complementary. If the natural enemy of science is inaccuracy or presumption, then the natural enemy of poetry is hypocrisy. To the extent that science and poetry keep inaccuracy, presumption and hypocrisy at bay, to that extent are they mutually beneficial ways of learning the world. The scientist brings us back to bedrock fact when our conclusions outstrip the evidence. The poet says, to paraphrase Hamlet's caution to Horatio, that there is more on earth than we think there is. The true scientist follows his curiosity wherever his hypotheses and experiments lead him, and he returns the wiser. A poet mysteriously creates wonder in a poem. Wisdom and wonder. Who can deny that we need them both?

5

Standpoint Eliot's; Outlook Mine

Rumor has it that Robert Frost was once informed by an exuberant student that there were more than 10,000 poets in the United States. What the student really meant was that there were allegedly more than 10,000 persons who claimed, according to a national survey, to be poets. Frost is reported to have smiled a dismissive smile and said, "Son, there haven't been 10,000 poets in the history of the world."

Frost seemed to know instinctively what T.S. Eliot understood critically, namely, that poetry is not a closet activity, that identifying oneself as a poet does not necessarily make it so, that there must eventually be some connection between the self-proclaimed poem and literature itself. In Eliot's language this meant and still means that individual talent exists within and derives its values from the literary tradition of which it is inescapably a part.

The reluctance of many "poets" to be aware of tradition and then to focus exclusively on their own "creativity" easily explains why there could be 10,000 or even 20,000 such "poets" in the land at any one time. The fact that they write what they consider to be poems seems to be enough for them to justify their claim. Their deliberate ignorance of tradition permits them to think that everything they do is original. In short, they write, but, as Stephen Spender remarked, they do not read. Of course, they themselves want desperately to be read, but, in Louis Simpson's words, why should anybody read them if they do not read anybody else? By the standards of such "poets," talent exists in a measureless vacuum, and any writer of what is assumed to be poetry can believe anything he wants to believe about himself.

In politics and war it has been said that one retains one's identity not by being more *against* what one is *against* but by being more *for* what one is *for*. What is true of politics and war is also true of literary criticism. In this respect Eliot's critical wisdom as well as his taste and patience have much to offer contemporary poets and critics not only vis-à-vis their recognition of tradition as a factor in determining talent but also in the meanings they attach to what poets are and what poetry should be.

In 1932 Eliot wrote that "some people who are inarticulate, may have a deeper and more discriminating sensibility than some others who can talk glibly about it; we must remember too that poetry is not written simply to provide material for conversation." Forewarned by Eliot that the meaning and experience of poetry "is only partially translatable into words," I propose to demonstrate that true poets (for Eliot as for the rest of us) are rare (sometimes one or two to a century) and that the appreciation of poetry derives from the "sum of experiences of good poems." What this means is that our ability to discern and appreciate true poets and their poems is directly proportionate to our reading or our hearing of good poems. The result of this effort inevitably develops not only a critical taste but also a critical standard. Thinking that such an effort is a waste of time frequently results in no taste or no standard at all, and Eliot warned of this when he wrote that "a person whose experience is limited is always liable to be taken in by the sham or the adulterate article; and we see generation after generation of untrained readers being taken in by the sham and the adulterate in its own time—indeed preferring them, for they are more easily assimilable than the genuine article."

Some years ago I was invited to speak to a class of fifth graders about poetry. I began by asking the pupils what they thought poetry was. One boy answered that "poetry happened when you picked your best words and put feeling into them." I was immediately reminded of Eliot's description of poetry as "the best words in the best arrangement." Even though Eliot had not included "feeling" in the description, and even though he had referred pejoratively elsewhere to everyone's need to deal with "undisciplined squads of emotion," I felt that his having said that the "business of the poet is not to find new emotions, but to use the ordinary ones and, in working them into poetry, to express feelings" places him squarely on the side of feeling as a poetic element. And, of course, he had also written that poetic achievement is "the emotional equivalent of thought," and he consistently believed that it was far more difficult to express precise emotion than to express precise thought. I write these qualifications on Eliot's behalf only to show that he was not an enemy of feeling in his various essays on the nature of poetry. And yet his very stance as a critic placed him on the side of restraint rather than indulgence in the expression of feeling, but more of this later.

But feeling and word-arrangement notwithstanding, the essence of what distinguished a poet for Eliot was sensibility, the whole of a poet's capacity to experience reality. He spoke glowingly of the sensibilities of Dante, Milton and particularly Donne and Dryden. They had the capacity of felt thought and not the poetic fault of feeling and thinking separately, resulting in what Eliot identified as a "disassociation of sensibility." While those possessed of a unified sensibility could devour any kind of experience, and while "a thought to Donne was an experience" that "modified his sensibility," those in whom sensibility was lacking or split or compartmentalized were incapable of such a transfiguration. The poet of fractured sensibility might very well write a poem of technical excellence, but the feeling would not be of a quality comparable to that created by a unified sensibility, and that linguistic excellence or technical virtuosity would not be organic to the feeling but separate from or imposed upon it. For evidence Eliot cited Gray's "Elegy in a Country Churchyard" as being cruder than Marvell's "To His Coy Mistress." After reading both poems in this light, I found that Gray's poem was "cruder" inasmuch as it realized itself in a series of moralizing and sentimental vignettes while the energy of Marvell's syllogistic "proposition" was inherent in the very spinning out of the poem and was co-terminous with it. And I concluded that Eliot's view of sensibility implied an absence of vacuums in a poet's style and that a poem emanating from such a sensibility gave the reader or listener the sense that each word was being created from an evolving inner principle or form. Gray's "Elegy in a Country Churchyard" must have impressed Eliot as a poem willed into being rather than a poem spun from the seed of its own inspiration. Indeed this view is confirmed by Walter Jackson Bate, who stressed Eliot's irritation caused by the "absence of fertility and reach of metaphor, and of analytic intellectuality in the verse of Gray." If one reads both Gray's poem and Marvell's fairly, Eliot's irritation seems justified. A verse or two can be deleted from Gray's poem without mortal damage being done; the same cannot be said of Marvell's poem. Gray's poem would also qualify as a poem emanating from a "disassociation of sensibility." However faithfully Gray observed rhyme schemes and the discipline of quatrains, the poem as a whole lacks whatever it is that obedience to organic form gives a poem. The reader comes away from the poem not with a sense of life but with the experience that he has read a commentary on life. In a poem resulting from a unified sensibility, we have the feeling as readers that the poet is creating or discovering his meaning as he goes, that he is following where the poem leads. The poem thus grows by obedience to its own laws and its own inner imperatives. This is as much a principle of life as it is of artistic creation. In language that Aristotle himself might have used, Eliot wrote in this regard: "We can only say that a poem, in some sense, has its own life; that it parts from something quite different from a body of neatly ordered biographical data; that the feeling, or emotion or vision, resulting from the poem is something quite different from the feeling or emotion or vision in the mind of the poet."

If sensibility for Eliot is what makes a poet a poet, then sensibility is proper to the reader's essence as well. The true reader is an appreciator, and sensibility is the key to appreciation —sensibility and the taste that coexists with and because of it. The indispensability of sensibility is especially apparent when a reader reads a poet whose work had not yet been commented on by critics. In such cases the reader has made his own discovery and must make a judgment as to the value of the work that he has just discovered. "When you read new poetry," Eliot wrote in an essay on minor poetry, "poetry by someone whose name is not yet widely known, someone whom the reviews have not yet passed, you are exercising or should be exercising your own taste. There is nothing else to go by. The problem is not, as it appears to many readers, that of trying to like something you don't, but leaving your sensibility free to react naturally." And later in the same essay he added, "I need time in order to know what I really felt at the moment. And that feeling is not a judgment of greatness or importance: it is an awareness of *genuineness*."

These lucid sentences have always struck me as being as much a matter of common as of literary sense. It boils down to what Emerson stressed in "Self-Reliance," the need to fall back on the bedrock credentials of one's self and one's own discriminations. Not long ago I found myself in the position of Eliot's reader of "new" poetry when I opened a book by a contemporary American poet named Donald Finkel. Among the poems was one called "Oracle":

> It is I, Orpheus, speaking through a mouthful of dust;
> to hell with Apollo, I can keep still no longer.
> Listen, Finkel, stop piecing me together
> in your bounding iambics. Besides, you read too much;
>
> the tune the stones will dance to is not in the books.
> Inside your wife is sleeping, with fine long legs,
> whom Hades has not yet noticed. While there is time,
> get off your ass and make the most of her.

At first reading I felt that this was a well-turned poem. I liked it.
But somehow with each subsequent reading it became less impres-
sive, and I tried to understand why. Let me say first that its waning
impressiveness was not due to the word "ass" in the last line of the
poem. Even though an ass is by definition a limited target, poetry
is certainly able to accommodate it. Granting Finkel the right of
impersonating Orpheus and having him speak in Finkelese, I find
that the last line, though intriguing at first reading, is at odds with
the poem's preceding whimsy and even the lyrical elegance of "Inside
your wife is sleeping, with fine long legs,/Whom Hades has not yet
noticed." The poem is like a song that ends on a flat note. The last
line is acceptable vernacular, but in my view it does not fit. It is as
if Finkel himself has burst into the poem and given Orpheus a line
that he, Finkel, wanted to hear. Whether this qualifies as crudeness
in Eliot's lexicon is impossible to know, but it so qualifies in mine. It
echoes something of Catullus, and yet that old rapscallion's language,
even when it was the language of a procurer, was always what you
expected from the start. In Finkel's poem the language of a procurer
seems not only out of place but at war with the tone and the oracular
candor of the rest of the poem.

   On the other hand, Robert Pack's "Prayer for Prayer," which is
also a dramatic monologue (the speaker is a woman), gives a portrait
of a marriage that silences us with its compassion and its conjugal
beauty. The aching concern—the human love, if you will—of the
wife for her husband makes the poem sound like a mid-marriage
vow or a renewal of a vow. It has that touch of the passionate and
the sacred that Finkel's poem has for a moment and then loses, and
the loss is apparent in the contrast of the two since both poems,
after all, do deal with the same subject.

> Darling, splitting the wood can wait until
> the wind dies down. I want to try to say
> what's troubling me, although we vowed before
> we married that we'd keep our own beliefs
> and let the children choose. They've left home now;

there's not much more that we can do for them;
it's you and me together, only us,
and I'm afraid you won't get into heaven,
not having turned to God. Without you, how
could I be happy there, unless God wills
that I forget this life? I don't want that!
The March sun hasn't thawed those icicles
gleaming along the edges of our roof;
perhaps this constant wind has numbed my faith.

I've never had to ask you this before,
but would you try to pray? Make up the words
if only for my sake; start thanking God
for daily things like breakfast oranges
heaped in the yellow bowl your mother painted—
a couple bathing in a waterfall—
our wedding gift of thirty years ago;
thank Him for splitting wood. You know I know
that even when you grumble, still it's work
you love. Nothing I do will feel complete
until I've given thanks for doing it,
so that I'm not alone: like thanking you
for thanking me when I prepare a meal
adds grace to grace. That's not a phrase you'd use;
you would prefer to hold some meanings back:
"Grace is not fattening, how can it hurt?"
but what we feel is not so far apart,
though maybe it's the very space God wants
to test us with? My mother used to say:
"You cannot cling to what you love with all
your strength; God made some special part of us
for letting go." I understood her when
our children left, and I can almost hear
the spaces where they were. Maybe sorrow
is allowed in heaven, so God won't have to
cancel human love by making us forget?

I won't forget, not willingly; one day
in paradise, watching the clouds, I'd think
of you standing beside the frozen stream,
eyeing the wood still to be split, and stacked,
and I'd be back on earth—at least at heart.
God means for marriages to end with death,
but after that the Bible isn't clear.
Perhaps God's love begins where human love
completes itself, and yet I'll never tire
of the past we've shared. I know you'll promise me
you'll try to pray and then you'll ask the Lord
to help me find the strength to give up prayer—
as if God would enjoy our joke; you'll swear:
"By yonder icicle, I'll love the world until
it does me in!" Thinking is the problem;
we can't escape the sorrow of an end
without an end, death going on and on.
Although you never speak of it, I know
your father died while he was splitting wood;
your mother's telling always starts the same:
"Some snow had fallen on his knitted hat..."
as if for her all time had stopped. Maybe
that is what heaven's like? She seems to smile,
and then the age-lines darken in her face.

Darling, I know you know something in me
approves your laughing at my need to pray.
By yonder icicle, what human love
allows, we have! But don't stand grinning with
that orange in your mouth as if you were
some sacrificial pig! Go split more wood
while I put dinner on; listen to God's
silences even as the wind blows through
the icicles and piles snow by our shed;
we may be in for quite a night of it.

I do not include my commentary on these two poems by Finkel and Pack as matters extraneous to this essay, one of whose stated purposes is to consider certain criteria basic to Eliot's critical philosophy and to explore their implications in practical criticism of certain contemporary poems. And I was happy to learn recently that my admiration of Eliot's criteria was shared in exactly the same spirit by William Stafford, a poet for whom I have the highest respect. "But in some strange way," Stafford wrote, "I feel that the influence of T.S. Eliot is more on other people than on current American poets. I see critics like markers in the channel, tugged by what they measure, but I see writers like minnows disporting themselves in flurries of action that avoid the current." Stafford's, I hasten to add, was not a voice in the wilderness in this connection. Robert Lowell's admiration for Eliot as a critic was exceeded only by his admiration for Eliot as a poet; he stated openly that he wept at Eliot's death and is known to have regarded *Four Quartets* as one of the major poetic achievements of our time. I do not include the endorsements of Stafford or Lowell as attempts to build up a majority of Eliot *confirmandi*; Eliot's comments on sensibility, tradition and individual talent would be valid even if they were rejected by all. But at a time when our poetic tastes are being dictated to and even imposed upon us by self-proclaimed arbiters of poetic worth, it is not only valuable but crucial to one's independence to make up one's own mind and not have it made up by someone else. And in this sense Eliot's insistence that reader and poet alike possess an "awareness of genuineness" in the midst of any literary experience is not a negligible caution. Otherwise editors of the newest anthologies or publicists or judges of the annual sweepstakes for poetry in the name of Joseph Pulitzer will impose their tastes upon us. And their taste, like public opinion of any sort, is only as good as its sources. And even here Eliot has a contribution to make. In an essay entitled "To Criticize the Critic," Eliot specified the dangers of listening to self-anointed critics. He identified, for example, the "Super-Reviewer, for he has often been the official critic for some magazine or newspaper, and the occasion for each of his contributions (is) the publication of some new book." The second critic—to-be-distrusted, according to Eliot, is the "Critic with Gusto ... the advocate of the authors whose work he expounds, authors who are sometimes the forgotten or the unduly despised." For Eliot such critics, as well as those in another group he calls the "Academic and the Theoretical," are men and women whose work is not a "by-product" of "creative activity" and whose criticism is often limited or made partisan by that fact alone. In other words, their critical view is either myopic or else subsumed by the greater talent of the author they admire. In our own time such critics have extolled the surrealism of a poet like Charles Simic (a neo-surrealist if he is a surrealist at all) when the historical reasons for the birth of surrealism (like dada-ism) are long since past. Similarly the work of John Ashbery for years received such immense praise that I re-read Ashbery and even attended one of his poetry readings to see what I was missing or indeed had missed. My initial instinct about Mr. Ashbery's lack of memorability did not change. I came away from both the reading and the hearing with the conviction that, if pressed, I would have a hard time quoting or wanting to quote one of Mr. Ashbery's lines, let alone one of his poems. These are scyth-ing statements, to be sure, but I purport them with all the fallibility at my command as well as with the conviction that what qualifies as "genuineness" to me would probably perplex Harold Bloom but that T.S. Eliot, whose magnanimity as a critic was exceeded only by his acumen, would have understood.

Let us return from an application of Eliot's principles to a few contemporary poems and poets to certain other of his observations about poetry and poets. I have already noted Eliot's insistence that the poet as a user of words is automatically in a tradition—the tradition of the language itself. His poetry, therefore, cannot be considered in isolation. In the English-speaking or English-using tradition this means that every poem must dine at the same table with the sonnets of Shakespeare, the third satire of John Donne, the monologues of Robert Browning, "The Broken Tower" of Hart Crane, and Robert Frost's "Death of the Hired Man" and "Home Burial." The works of preceding poets by their very presence create an ineluctable standard (not of imitation but of poetic worth) against which new work is measured. The poet (as well as the critic) must possess, therefore, a historical sense, which is acquired only by his familiarizing himself deeply with his predecessors, in order to know what is new, as well as a sense of the presence of the past in order to detect that timelessness in the new that will outlast the passing moment. "Tradition," wrote Eliot, "...cannot be inherited, and if you want it you must obtain it by great labour. It involves, in the first place, the historical sense, which we may call nearly indispensable to anyone who would continue to be a poet beyond his twenty-fifth year; and the historical sense which involves a perception not only of the pastness of the past, but of its presence; the historical sense compels a man to write not merely with his own generation in his bones, but with the feeling that the whole literature of Europe from Homer and within it the whole literature of his own country has a simultaneous existence and composes a simultaneous order." It is only in this way that a poet can be "very conscious of the main current, which does not always flow invariably through the most distinguished reputations." Or, I hasten to add, through the reputations of those chosen for emulation by their pushers for reasons that have little if anything to do with poetry. In our own decade and in the decades immediately preceding it, poets like Allen Ginsberg and Robert Bly and Amiri Baraka (formerly Le Roi Jones) have been praised for sociological, ideological or political reasons that had very little to do with the poetry they wrote, if poetry it was. Ginsberg was a phenomenon of his own creation, at best a traveling rhapsode whose public appearances and associations have given him an aura in the minds of some that is supposed to impress us as poetic. Robert Bly's poems and positions vis-à-vis the tragedy of Vietnam and his public poetry readings with or without masks were, like the minstrelsy of the same era, largely limited to the time that provoked them. And I write this while fully admiring Bly's excellent translations of Scandinavian poets, his theories of translation generally, and many of his own poems on the page. And once I heard Amiri Baraka address the national convention of Arab University Graduates in Southfield, Michigan, by stressing that he greeted them in the name of the oncoming revolution and bringing them greetings from his brothers in North Korea. The men and women in the audience, to whom the tradition of Arabic poetry spoke in more visceral and eternal terms, were singularly unimpressed. In fact they were bored and even embarrassed by Baraka whose blatant leftism they instantly perceived as the ideology it was and not the poetry it pretended to be.

I mention Ginsberg, Bly and Baraka here to indicate that their work on behalf of their specific causes did not subsume that cause or that ideology into poetry. All too often they wrote verse at the service of their cause of the moment, and the cause may well have been served at poetry's expense. Eliot wrote in the "The Social Function of Poetry" that "Bad verse may have a transient vogue when the poet is reflecting a popular attitude of the moment; but real poetry survives not only a change of popular opinion but the complete extinction of interest in the issues with which the poet was passionately concerned."

This is not to say that a poet should not be immersed in his time. Eliot continually emphasized that a poet's perception of his own time in relation to the "tradition principle" was what revealed the significance of the present to him. "What is to be insisted upon," Eliot wrote, "is that the poet must develop or procure the consciousness of the past and that he should continue to develop this consciousness throughout his career. What happens is a continual surrender of himself as he is at the moment to something which is more valuable." This is an important point. It explains what Eliot meant when he wrote that the writing of poetry demanded an extinction of personality, not as a conscious act but as something that the poet at the moment of inspiration accepted. It's what great actors do when they get "into the character" they're portraying. Their own personalities yield to the personality of the character; the result is "acting." I remember reading a piece by Garson Kanin a number of years ago where he described Spencer Tracy's first read-through of a script called *Pat and Mike*. Kanin described how Tracy and Katherine Hepburn were reading their respective parts aloud when, at a certain point, Tracy *became* Mike. Kanin could not say exactly when the transformation happened (it is as much a mystery as the writing of a poem is a mystery), but there was no doubt in his mind that it did happen.

So much then for Eliot's concept of poetry's essence and the poetic process and the few instances I've specified to relate these concepts to certain contemporary poets and practices. What of poetry's social function and social consequences? Here Eliot's conservatism and realism compelled him to ascribe to poetry rather modest goals. In "The Social Function of Poetry" he wrote that poetry's first function is simply to "give pleasure." He then added that a related function "is always the communication of some new experience, or some fresh understanding of the familiar, of the expression of something we have experienced but have no words for, which enlarges our consciousness or refines our sensibility." Then, after insisting that "no art is more stubbornly national than poetry," Eliot stressed that the "duty of the poet, as poet, is only indirectly to his people: his direct duty is to his language, first to preserve, and second to extend it. In expressing what other people feel he is also changing the feeling by making it more conscious; he is making people more aware of what they feel already, and therefore teaching them something about themselves. But he is not merely a more conscious person than the others; he is also individually different from other people, and from other poets too, and can make his readers share consciously in new feelings which they had not experienced before ... And in expressing them he is developing and enriching the language which he speaks."

Even though it is less messianic than Shelley's or Sidney's claims for poetry, Eliot's delineations of poetry's social function are certainly far removed from Auden's "Poetry makes nothing happen" (from "In Memory of W.B. Yeats"). Poetry cannot help but make something happen—not as politicians, social activists or revolutionaries would understand that phenomenon—but (the word keeps re-appearing as if to further underline its importance) at the level of sensibility—the poet's as well as the reader's. And again the importance of tradition can never be disregarded. The deeper the poet's sense of tradition—literary, linguistic and social—-the more compelling and transforming will be his poetry, the more his and his reader's sensibilities will be changed. It is not by accident that poets are among the first to feel the wrath of tyrants or totalitarians. Poets say what others only see; they confirm a vision that is the province of human and not governmental truth since it springs from the imagination. By killing or imprisoning them, tyrants hope to put out the very eyes of the population so that the vision of the tyrants and their vision alone prevails. To all such suppression poetry stands opposed, simply by being faithful to itself.

Let me now turn to the work of certain contemporary black poets and see how relevant some of Eliot's criteria are vis-à-vis poetry's social function. It is almost a matter of conventional wisdom to say that many black poets (particularly in the United States) write passionately (and with understandable reason) out of a sense of racial consciousness alone. Although Richard Wright warned his peers of the limitations that would result from writing only out of racial consciousness, his warning has been frequently disregarded. Many poems are written in what has been called "black English" so that they are intended often by black writers for black readers and against Caucasians. The poems are intended as communications, not communions, and in some instances are synonymous with ammunition. Some of the poems of Gwendolyn Brooks are of this character as are most of the poems of Etheridge Knight. Despite the awards that Ms. Brooks and Mr. Knight have received, my own view is that their work in this regard does not possess the staying power of poets like Robert Hayden, Langston Hughes and Derek Walcott, and the reason is that the latter poets simply have a better command of language and a deeper sense of tradition. Derek Walcott told me once that a number of black students in New York took him to task when he told them that they needed to steep themselves in the literature of England and America since they intended, after all, to write in the English (or, respecting Mencken's distinction, American) language. The students retorted that they were not interested in doing so since they had no desire to become proficient in the language of those who were responsible for the oppression of black people. Walcott, who authored the prophetic line..."We are no one or we are a nation," is not a man to whom oppression is foreign, but his literary sense transcends that. Like Hayden and Hughes, he is able to write in patois when he chooses to do so, but he is also able to express a broader sensibility in the language that is the common property of oppressor and oppressed alike. Walcott's transfigurative power as a poet for all readers and not only members of his race or region is thus directly proportionate to his mastery of the language that is common to all. Eliot suggested as much when he wrote that if a "... poet is to learn how to use words in our time, he must devote close study to those who have used them best in their time; to those who, in their own day, have made the language new." And he buttressed this point in "The Use of Poetry and the Use of Criticism": "And when I speak of modern poetry as being extremely critical, I mean that the contemporary poet, who is not merely a composer of graceful verses,——is forced to ask himself such questions as 'what is poetry for?'; not merely 'what am I to say' but rather 'how and to whom am I to say it?' We have to communicate—if it is communication, for the word may be in question—an experience which is not an experience in the ordinary sense for it may only exist, formed out of many personal experiences ordered in some way, which may be very different from the way of valuation of practical life, in the expression of it. If *poetry* is a form of 'communication,' yet that which is to be communicated is the poem itself..." Robert Hayden's "Those Winter Sundays" is certainly a poem of this type. There are no racial pros and cons, no stoppings at the epidermal frontiers, no hidden defiances, and every human being is instantly in communion with its familial theme:

> Sundays too my father got up early
> and put his clothes on in the blueblack cold,
> then with cracked hands that ached
> from labor in the weekday weather made
> banked fires blaze. No one ever thanked him.

I'd wake and hear the cold splintering, breaking.
When the rooms were warm, he'd call,
and slowly I would rise and dress,
fearing the chronic angers of that house,

speaking indifferently to him,
who had driven out the cold
and polished my good shoes as well.
What did I know, what did I know
of love's austere and lonely offices?

Passing from Hayden's beautiful lyric to a poem by Derek Walcott only confirms the point that an awareness of tradition, of history, of politics, of art, of societies other than one's own, re-created through the talent of a visionary poet, is capable of creating a poem that can stop anyone, regardless of race, in his very tracks. Here is the XXIII poem from Walcott's *Midsummer* that is lyric in spirit but epic in implication. In this poem Walcott uses a race riot in England as a basis for a comment on the biracial consequences of nineteenth-century imperialism. The mention of Caliban at the poem's conclusion links it with *The Tempest*, but Setebos has been transformed into an English backalley. Despite (or perhaps because of) its brevity the poem seems to explode on the page. It creates the effect of instantaneity, but it is an instantaneity that is rife with echoes. It confirms Eliot's insistence that the deeper the poet is immersed in his time (with the sensibility and the traditional sense to match), the better the chances that his poetry will be prophetic of his time. The poet is made synonymous with a seer, someone who sees and says what others merely observe or do not see at all.

With the stampeding hiss and scurry of green lemmings,
midsummer's leaves race to extinction like a roar
of a Brixton riot tunnelled by water hoses;
they seethe toward autumn's fire—it is in their nature,

being man as well as leaves, to die for the sun.
The leaf stems tug at their chains, the branches bending
like Boer cattle under Tory whips that drag every wagon
nearer to apartheid. And, for me, that closes
the child's fairy tale of an antic England—fairy rings,
thatched cottages fenced with dog roses,
a green gale lifting the hair of Warwickshire.
I was there to add some color to the British theater.
"But blacks can't do Shakespeare, they have no experience."
This was true. Their thick skulls bled with rancor
you could trace to the Sonnets, or the Moor's eclipse.
Praise had bled my lines white of any more anger,
and snow had inducted me into white fellowships,
while Calibans howled down the barred streets of an empire
that began with Caedmon's raceless dew, and is ending
in the alleys of Brixton, burning like Turner's ships.

Here, in conjunction with and in reference to Walcott's poem, is as good a place as any to consider Eliot's concept of the "objective correlative." In a frequently quoted passage from his essay on *Hamlet*, Eliot wrote: "The only way of expressing emotion in the form of art is by finding an 'objective correlative', in other words, a set of objects, a situation, a chain of events which shall be the formula of that particular emotion; such as that when the external facts, which must terminate in sensory experience, are given, the emotion is immediately invoked." This has always impressed me as being a more academic way of stating what Hemingway said when he stressed that the essential element in writing is to describe what you felt in action—the particular things that evoke feeling—so that the reader, in the act of reading the description, can feel something akin to what the writer himself felt during the experience itself. For me the key phrase in Eliot's concept is his insistence that "the only way of expressing emotion *in the form of art* (italics mine) is by finding an 'objective correlative.'" This means that the poem as an art form must carry its own emotional weight through its own inner workings, association, symbols, overtones, connotations and sound. Poets that lack this creative capacity may express emotion, but it is not "emotion in the form of art." Supplying numerous exclamation points or heightened capitalizations or giving way to emotional drooling or emotional diarrhea does not fill in the gap. The power of Walcott's poem, for example, is in the restraint and economy of its frames of reference. The references to "riot," "apartheid," Shakespeare's "Sonnets," *Othello* and *The Tempest* inevitably place the race-riot and the violence of the "water hoses" against the permanent England that exists in Shakespeare's language, in Caedmon, in Turner. The contrast thus makes the poet's affection for an "antic England" appear like a "fairy tale," an illusion, a sham. Each time the poem is re-read the contrasts become more apparent, and the more the poem grows in its reverberations. History is there; man's inhumanity to man is there; Cain and Abel are there; the current manifestations of prejudice and hatred are there; the conflagration in "the alleys of Brixton" and its linkage to the flaming of "Turner's ships" are there, poetically creating a different art form than Turner's but more vivid as a result of the association. Above all, there is maturity in the poem. One trusts the poet emotionally in the context of the poem itself. This is not the same as trusting the poet's feeling as a man; it means trusting the feelings evoked by the language of the poem, and, from an artistic point of view, this is by far more important.

The concept of the "objective correlative" is crucial to Eliot's aesthetic. In addition to saving poetry from overt confessionalism, it gives depth to Eliot's delineation of what he calls the "three voices" of poetry: "The first voice is the voice of the poet talking to himself—or to nobody. The second is the voice of the poet addressing an audience whether large or small. The third is the voice of the poet when he attempts to create a dramatic character speaking in verse; when he is saying, not what he would say in his own person, but only what he can say within the limits of one imaginary character addressing another imaginary character."

Even though Eliot admitted that the three voices "are most often found together," he insisted earlier in the same essay that underlying

the writing of poetry in whatever voice is the effort of the poet to
"achieve clarity for himself, to assure himself that the poem is the
right outcome of the process that has taken place. The most bun-
gling form of obscurity is that of the poet who has not been able
to express himself to himself; the shoddiest form is found when
the poet is trying to persuade himself that he has something to say
when he hasn't." Eliot's classical tastes and standards prevented him
from regarding poetry as mere effluvia; he knew that clarity—artistic
clarity—from a man who has something to say is the criterion that
poets cannot abrogate. By identifying the only three voices that any
poet can assume when writing a poem, Eliot kept the act of criti-
cal evaluation where it belonged—on the poem. We can, therefore,
conclude at this point that, according to Eliot, a poet "talking to
himself" or to "an audience" or in a "dramatic character" must still be
evaluated within the tradition of literature itself. That tradition will
impose its own standards of excellence upon the poem or poet seek-
ing to affect that tradition in one of three forms of poetic utterance
(or a combination of all three). The evaluation of that experience is
what literary criticism is all about. And being a literary critic is, as
I have already noted, what makes independent judgment possible.
Eliot emphasized the point by stating that, "Literary criticism is a
distinctive activity of the civilized mind." And all who love poetry
and believe in its indispensability to the fullness of human life must
develop that quality of mind by making up their own minds since
literary criticism, as Craig LaDriere wrote years ago, is "judgment,
not a memory of judgment."

The proper conclusion to this essay requires that all the aforemen-
tioned principles be related to several important observations that
are included in Eliot's "Religion and Literature." These observations
are derivative of two principles that Eliot stressed in that essay. They
complete his entire critical philosophy and, quite literally, save it
from semanticism, aestheticism, neo-classicism or even secularism.
The first axiom is Eliot's insistence that "Literary criticism should be
completed by criticism from a definite ethical or theological stand-
point." He clarified this by adding that "The greatness of literature

cannot be determined solely by literary standards; though we must remember that whether it is literature or not can be determined only by literary standards." By establishing a direct association between literature and theology, Eliot eschewed Matthew Arnold's error of ascribing totally to poetry what could only be ascribed to religion. Eliot's concern is not to polarize poetry and religion but to accentuate their interdependence. In short, he asked of literature as a whole, and of the "superior amusement" that is poetry in particular, an accounting of its total view of man, which is not only a theological question but which returns us to the sensibility of the poet as much as to the fact of the poem in question. Why? For Eliot the answer was a simple one, however disputable it might have been and may still be to others. The poetry of Shakespeare and Dante appealed to him because it offered a saner attitude toward the mystery of life as he perceived it. He made this the cornerstone of all his practical criticism. As a practical critic he knew that all criticism was meant to end in judgment, and he stressed that as judging practical critics we "need to be acutely aware of two things at once: of 'what we like' and of 'what we ought to like.'" As a Christian Eliot naturally felt "the duty of maintaining consciously certain standards and criteria over and above those applied by the rest of the world." He did not mean that this should limit critics to polemical or devotional poetry for their "superior amusement." He meant that he preferred a "literature, which would be unconsciously rather than deliberately or defiantly, Christian."

By way of personal summation I would like to quote several poems that have for years impressed me as literature in the sense in which Eliot understood the term. As presumptuous as it may appear for me to do so, it permits me to extend my theoretical consideration of Eliot's aesthetic into practical terms. One of the ways in which the genuineness of a poem reveals itself to me is its defiance at being contained or framed by the page on which it is printed. Like a surprise it exceeds what we may have expected. It is more than the sum of its parts. It suggests more than it means. It cannot be reduced to a rationale. This places it on the side of mystery, and mystery is for me a spiritual or, if you will, a religious matter. The following poems illustrate the point. The first is entitled "The Poem" by W.S. Merwin.

> Coming late, as always,
> I am trying to remember what I almost heard.
> The light avoids my eye.
>
> How many times have I heard the locks close
> And the lark take the keys
> And hang them in heaven.

The second is "Unsatisfied Desire" by William Bronk.

> However beautiful I think you are
> I am not content to let it end there.
> And, oh, you are beautiful even to the extent
> that your imperfections insist that beautiful
> is not in being perfect but in such faults
> —shall we call them faults?—as your imperfection has.
> And I could agree: those faults are beautiful.
>
> There is a world of possibilities;
> also, there are things not possible.
> Desires satisfied set us apart
> in a reciprocal pattern self-contained
> and not containing more. It replicates,
> trapped in a world of possibilities,
> alone, where it is the only possible.
>
> I have seen such beautiful things in the world which, apart
> from desire, I should never have seen. I bless desire,
> I bless that fault: that, in its offering
> denying us all, denies us nothing,
> offers the world to us, not to have.

I do not find this type of excellence in the work of John Ashbery. And I single him out deliberately because his multiple awards and other recognitions have established him as a kind of role model for younger poets. Let us put aside for the moment that the has been extolled by writers like Donald Barthelme and Doris Brownwich and that he has received the National Book Award, the Pulitzer Prize and a host of other citations. After reading and re-reading Ashbery, I could not rid myself of the notion that he is simply a linguistic juggler. There are lines in his poems that are as crowded with words in dazzling combinations as certain non-representative paintings are crowded with color. But is poetry so much dazzle? And is it critically justifiable to pass off many of Ashbery's lines as "flutterings...of the fledged imagination" (in the language of John Hollander) when the lines are simply obscure? To support my claim I cite the following poem, "Bird's-Eye View of the Tool and Die Co.," as a fairly typical example of Ashbery's style.

> For a long time I used to get up early.
> 20-30 vision, hemorrhoids intact, he checks into the
> Enclosure of time familiarizing dreams
> For better or worse. The edges rub off,
> The slant gets lost. Whatever the villagers
> Are celebrating with less conviction is
> The less you. Index of own organ-music playing,
> Machinations over the architecture (too
> Light to make much of a dent) against meditated
> Gang-wars, ice cream, loss, palm terrain.
>
> Under and around the quick background
> Surface is improvisation. The force of
> Living hopelessly backward into a past of striped
> Conversations. As long as none of them ends this side
> Of the mirrored desert in terrorist chorales.
> The finest car is as the simplest home off the coast
> Of all small cliffs too short to be haze. You turn

> To speak to someone beside the dock and the lighthouse
> Shines like garnets. It has become a stricture.

I have read critics who claim to be "beguiled" and "bedazzled" by
Ashbery's use of language. But just take a line like "The finest car is
as the simplest home off the coast/ Of all small cliffs too short to
be haze." What does it mean? What is the point of view of a poem
that begins in the first person, shifts to the third, shifts again to
the second, proceeds into abstruse descriptive passages and ends in
the second person. But why go on? Let us pass to the more serious
question of quoting those poems that seem to me to fulfill Eliot's
criteria of being poems we "ought to like." They not only work as
poems, but they impress me as extending and enhancing the tradi-
tion of which they are part. They go beyond confessionalism and
hermeticism to evoke values that are universally apprehensible. In
short, they convince me of their poetic validity. The "objective cor-
relatives" hold up, creating on the page a set of images and tropes
that evoke the very feelings the poet must have had when he was
originally inspired. The first of these poems is John Ciardi's "In
Place of a Curse."

> At the next vacancy for God, if I am elected,
> I shall forgive last the delicately wounded
> who, having been slugged no harder than anyone else,
> never got up again, neither to fight back,
> nor to finger their jaws in painful admiration.
>
> They who are wholly broken, and they in whom
> mercy is understanding, I shall embrace at once
> and lead to pillows in heaven. But they who are
> the meek by trade, baiting the best of their betters
> with the extortions of a mock-helplessness
>
> I shall take last to love, and never wholly.
> Let them all into Heaven—I abolish Hell—

but let it be read over them as they enter:
"Beware the calculations of the meek, who gambled nothing,
gave nothing, and could never receive enough."

The second poem is "Work" by William Stafford. Stafford's poem,
like Ciardi's, confirms a previously quoted reference that Eliot made
when he said that a "thought to Donne was an experience; it modified
his sensibility." My reaction to "In Place of a Curse" and to "Work"
is identical to Eliot's reaction to Donne. Each poem is a solution
of sorts for the poet (you can almost feel it as you experience each
line), but the act of solution and the act of poetry seem one and
the same, and this is as it should be.

> There is a dream going on while I am awake.
> Because I must pay attention to what
> is happening around me, I am unconscious
> of the dream. When I sleep, the daylight
> things fade out and the perpetual dream
> surfaces fully and is memorable.
> When I die, the dream is the only
> thing left. It balloons and fills the world.
>
> As a writer, I coax partly into action
> that internally coherent, silent story.
> I let my conscious life yield a little,
> and a little more, and occasionally a great way,
> to my best needs and hopes: whatever
> I mean by my best, whatever I mean
> by my judgments of the happenings around me,
> that center and guide is invited to have its way.
>
> For intervals then, throughout our lives
> we savor a concurrence, the great blending
> of our chance selves with what sustains
> all chance. We ride the wave and are

the wave. And with renewed belief
inner and outer we find our talk
turned into prayer, our prayer into truth:
for an interval, early, we become at home in the world.

To further buttress my personal selections of poems that, in Eliot's words, we "ought to like," I could quote poems by Richard Wilbur, Galway Kinnell, Linda Pastan, Naomi Shihab Nye, Peter Makuck, and Stanley Kunitz as well as such foreign poets as Seamus Heaney, George Seferis, Adonis, and Pablo Neruda. But I think the examples I've given are sufficient to illustrate my tastes, and I am egotist enough to suggest that these and Eliot's tastes are not divergent, at least in principle. My critical purpose is the same as his, namely, "to help the reader to understand and enjoy." And my emphasis on the order of literary diet is the same, namely, an avoidance of false garnish or junk meals in favor of the real nourishment of the imagination and the sustenance of man in his totality. "The author of a work of the imagination," Eliot wrote, "is trying to affect us wholly, as human beings, whether he knows it or not; and we are affected by it, as human beings, whether we intend it or not. I suppose that everything we eat has some other effect upon us than merely the pleasure of taste and mastication; it affects us during the process of assimilation and digestion; and I believe that exactly the same is true of anything we read."

6

The Poetry of Anemia

"For poetry makes nothing happen..." Ever since W.H. Auden wrote this ironically vapid line in his otherwise memorable elegy for William Butler Yeats, numerous American and British poets have been writing in ways to prove him correct. Part of the fault can be traced to the influence of Auden himself on these writers. Putting aside his astuteness as a critic and his significant career as a judge for the Yale Younger Poets Series, he remained a poet whose poems often seemed to be commentaries on the emotions he evoked and not expressions of the emotions themselves. His intellectual brilliance made (and still makes) many of his admirers and poetic imitators ignore the basic deficiency that this tendency created in his poems. This deficiency is an absence of passion. Poetry written in this vein is not the "true voice of feeling" that Herbert Read said it should be but frequently the mere versification of thought. It conveys the after-the-fact wisdom of the commentator, not the experiencer itself, even though all poets know that they must be experiencers with the ability to re-create their experiences in words that enable others to feel what they have felt (as opposed to telling them what they have felt). Lacking this, they lack what we go to poetry to find.

In the case of Auden and those of his emulators who have imitated his style but lack his brilliance, we are confronted by some of the most "intellectual" poetry of our time but also some of the least passionate. The poetry is ideational, not emotional, but these poets ignore the fact that what is important in poetry is not the idea *per se* (we read philosophy for that) but the *experience* of the idea. The early poems of Randall Jarrell, for example, reveal this weakness. It was not until Jarrell pulled out of his early Audenism that he was able to write some of the most ineradicable poems that we have about war, loneliness, women and aging.

If poetry of this character is not mere verse or consciously wrought prosody, it is in essence the poetry of erudition or, from the perspective of its lack of passion, the poetry of anemia. It glimmers in its finery, but it ignores the fact that the body is more than the raiment, and the spirit is more than the body. Here the body and spirit of poetry seem relegated to secondary or tertiary status, and what is left is facility. In Castiglione's day this would have been called the talent of Euphues. It our time it does not have a name, but it abounds.

What is behind this outpouring of polished vacuity? Why does a poet like John Ashbery occupy such a central place in the contemporary pantheon of American poetry (and who created such an anointing in the first place?) while better poets such as Louis Simpson and Philip Booth receive nowhere near the attention they merit? How did such a sorry state of poetic affairs happen? Can it be attributable entirely to the influence of pontificators like Helen Vendler and her Manhattan counterparts? And, if so, why have they been able to get away with it for so long to the ultimate detriment of the catholicity that is proper to poetry's nature and to the adulterating of the tastes of young student writers to whom such poetasting is held up as admirable and worthy of imitation. It parallels the bad gospel of some years ago when young women at Bennington and elsewhere were told that the fate of Anne Sexton and Sylvia Plath foretold the inevitable fate of the female poet in America. Denise

Levertov made short work of the idiocy at the time, suggesting that the lives of these two women were not shortened by poetry but rather lengthened and enriched by it.

The case of John Ashbery is as good a place to pick an argument as any. The associative way he writes, as I have suggested in the previous essay, has given birth to the glacial theory of writing, which means that the poem goes wherever the associations go. The result is a surface that is a mile wide and a half-inch deep. Here is but one example called "Sand Pail."

> Process
> of a red stripe through much whiplash
> of environmental sweepstakes misinterprets
> slabs as they come forward. A
> footprint
> directs traffic in the center
> of flat crocus plaza as the storm
> incurves on this new position. Why
> are there developments?
> A transparent shovel paves, "they" say,
> residual elastic fetters
> pictures of the moments
> brought under the sand.

In the previous chapter, I tried to find something intelligible and "feelable" in another Ashbery poem called "Bird's-Eye View of the Tool and Dye, Co." and finally gave up. "Sand Pail" fills me with the same why-bother attitude.

Compare "Sand Pail" with either of the following poems of Louis Simpson and Philip Booth respectively to see the difference between true poetic vision and tiddly-winks. Simpson's brief poem is entitled "The Bazuft."

In Persia, there's a wandering tribe—
every year they come to a river,

the Bazuft, they all have to cross.
Those who don't are left behind.

The sun warm on the mat, the sound
of the sheep-bell a long way off.

The poem has an almost Japanese subtlety to it. The river called Bazuft
becomes the dividing line between life and death. The ones who are
"left behind" resign themselves to the "sun warm on the mat" and to
the departing "sheep-bell a long way off" as the tribe and its flocks
move on. The poem is an epitaph to the old, the enfeebled and the
abandoned, but the poignancy is delicate, almost too gentle.

Philip Booth's poem "Zeros" reads like an epitaph to our age, to
a falsely protective way of thinking, to the vices that we have come
to regard as virtues.

Three zeros coming up,
as the odometer turns
toward its new thousand.
Old movies, cars pushing
2002, the number maybe
we'll get to, maybe we'll
not. As if numbers were
our destination, as if
we weren't close to lost.
As if it didn't matter
how we've already poisoned
the planet, invaded lovers,
borne generations of micro
chips, wired our lives to
suicide bombs, and still
told ourselves, year after

penultimate year, that there
will be survivors, that we'll
be the heroes who'll last.

The conclusion I have long since drawn from looking at Ashbery's work and that of his imitators is that words are not supposed to have any relation to people and the things of this world but only to one another. In other words, the most important dimension of language (meaning) is removed from the writing of poetry, and one is left with the equivalent of fingerpainting. Such an aesthetic is not only shallow but also fundamentally and mischievously wrong. Words are not dominoes. They mean; they have references, histories, overtones, undertones. They are meant to say what we see and feel, and they remain one of the few ways we have of expressing what is in our heads and hearts. Arbitrarily consigning them to the world of meaninglessness does violence to the very nature and purpose of language. It is also self-defeating because it stands between language and its true destiny. Small wonder that Ashbery has imitators; anybody with the right knack can create this kind of verbiage, but those who do so create an affront to poetry and, simultaneously, do violence to whatever real talent they do possess.

A different but no less fatuous aberration is "poetry" that is thinly disguised advocacy. Where "finger-painting" in verse is obscure and usually pointless, advocative "poetry" is strident and direct. Some readers (usually the easily excitable) are drawn to such verse for the same reason that they are drawn to some of our more unsubtle comedians who "let it all hang out." Occasionally it associates itself with political or social movements, i.e., environmental concerns, anti-apartheid movements, AIDS marches, women's liberation and so on.

If shouted advocacy is poetry, then cheerleading is poetry. Unfortunately, many foreigners often conclude that such "poetry "—because it is the loudest—is in the mainstream of our literary tradition. (For a time the Beats had this reputation, but who reads them any more except as a kind of historical parallel to Woodstock, which has been equally overrated as a transfigurative force in mid-century American mores). Allen Ginsberg, for example, made a career of traveling and reading his advocacies abroad, and in many countries he was the only poet from America that the native population knew so that these people drew their conclusions about poetry in the United States from this one example.

Regrettably, this is not unlike the conclusions drawn by foreigners about the United States when their only source of information has come from exported Hollywood films. But apart from cultural parallels, the stridency of such advocative verse does not disguise the fact that it, like much modern advertising, borrows tropes from poetry but is not poetry at all. Indignation and anger are not substitutes for inspiration. Rhetoric is not poetry. Beneath all the bluster and public hamming-it-up there is the same spiritual anemia that I referred to earlier. The poet of fingerpainting has nothing to say but disguises it with cleverness. The authors of the poetry of advocacy talk big but imagine small.

A deeper reason for the indifference of the public to true poetic utterance is their suspicion that they think poetry—like some examples of contemporary art—is best left to the initiated few. And since the initiated few (whoever they are) are quite few indeed, why should the general public care about poetry at all? Seen against the background of American reading habits, this is hardly shocking. Jerzy Kosinski once cited a survey that revealed that 50% of those surveyed admitted that they had not read a single book during the preceding year. Of the remaining 50%, 38% admitted to having read one book. This means that only 12% read more than one book during the time period in question. Of this minority consider how many actually read a book of poems, and you can readily understand why publishers (if they are telling the truth) are modestly happy if a book of poems sells between 2000 and 3000 hardback copies on the average. One can only imagine the effect that this survey would have had on one articulate surgeon who wrote recently that no person can call himself educated unless he has read more than fifty books a year *outside* of his field.

Taking advantage of the shameful reading habits of Americans is hardly an excuse of the poets of anemia to go on writing what the public won't read anyway. But that seems to be the case. Poets who are "pushed" by this or that publishing house are often so hermetic as to be inaccessible to any but their own cronies, and thus those few who take poetry seriously turn to Dante or Shakespeare or Donne or Hopkins or Dickinson or Frost to nourish themselves and let the newly anointed vanish in the withering test of time. One can even argue that Shakespeare is in this sense more contemporary than various winners of the Pulitzer Prize and other national prizes, but what's the use? A good poem will survive and create its own audiences regardless, and that's the top and bottom of it. All of these articles about the "state" and "direction" of American poetry in the sixties, seventies, eighties or nineties, about the need for "expansionism" or for the revival of a narrative voice are just so much space-fillers, no more.

There is no such thing as a "state" or "direction" of poetry being written now or at any time. There are only good poems written here and there and now and then by specific men and women who have specific (usually accidental and largely irrelevant) addresses on this planet, some of which are in the United States. Notice that I said "poems" and not poets" in this context. Let me explain. I think that Robert Pack's "Prayer for Prayer" from his earlier *Voices in a Single Tree* will last as long as John Donne's "A Valediction Forbidding Mourning." I think that Maxine Kumin's "We Stood There Singing" from *Nurture* is one of the most symphonic poems I have read in some time. Charles Simic can write a diamond of a poem like "Fear" ("Fear passes from man to man/Unknowing/As one leaf passes its shudder/To another./All at once the whole tree is trembling/And there is no sign of the wind.") while simultaneously writing numerous poems in the tradition of Mallarmé and other symbolists and surrealists that do not tap his real talent.

Another prevalent vice that does a disservice to poetry and the readers of poetry who actually do exist "out there" is the palsy-walsy system that seems to operate vis-à-vis publishing houses and the poetry-award juries. Too often, for instance, one publisher's "in-house" authors will be prevailed upon to write congratulatory blurbs to be used to promote a book by a new poet being added to the publisher's list. How seriously can these encomii be taken if they all have the consanguinity of ink upon them? And as for the poetry-award juries, who is prescient enough to say what favoritism is at work there? Considering that the external awards for poets are so few (apart from and inferior to the intrinsic award that every poet gives to himself when he has finished working on his own poem), one wonders why the lobbying and the behind-the scenes campaigns are so fierce.

A former judge on one of the Pulitzer committees in the 1970's told me that he became so indignant when he learned that his fellow jurors had determined and even announced a winner prior to the convening of the jury that he bollixed the whole process until a true consensus of all jurors could be reached. This award was then given justly to Robert Penn Warren.

Many have stated that the Pulitzers are not a reliable gauge in highlighting which poets are currently significant and which are not. Cummings, Jeffers and Ciardi, for example, were never chosen during their years of eligibility, and they seem to be head-and-shoulders over such Pulitzered writers as Audrey Wurdemann, Leonard Bacon, Peter Viereck and Phyllis McGinley. But then this award has a history that confirms periodic off-the-mark selections. Just look at the record. After the Pulitzers were established, it was belatedly conceded that something should be done for "verse." Wilbur Lucius Cross, a Professor in the Graduate School at Yale and later a Governor of Connecticut, became the chairman of the selection committee and held the chairmanship for twenty-five years. Lo and behold, the first dozen or so awardees were all from New England. One wonders why poets themselves never railed against this overt provincialism which, in different forms, continues to the present day. All too few question these goings-on. Why? For fear of offending those who are in a position to boost or break their careers, anthologizing their poems or fixing them up with a teaching post or a grant or some such? Is the politics of poetry more important finally than poetry itself? Philip Levine and Donald Hall have spoken up against such philistinism, but they are two among too many of the silent.

What the poetry of anemia has, of course, created is its own apologists. Thus we are treated to the arcane prose of the structuralists, the post-structuralists, constructionists, deconstructionists, modernists, Post-modernists, semanticists, linguists, followers of Barthes, Derrida and so forth. When one compares this outpouring with the lucid, personal essays that Mark Van Doren wrote about Shakespeare or the critical prose that T.S. Eliot wrote throughout his life or the literary honesty of Louis Simpson or Robert Pack, one wonders what has happened to the honest act of literary appreciation.

The ultimate result of clique-ishness of style and outlook where poets in effect write versified, critical or promotional valentines for one another, where the fantastical is mistaken for the truly imaginative, where bad poetry does its best to drive out good poetry and where poets who should be heard and read and are not is that poetry itself and the poetry-needing public are the losers. In a sense this essay has been more iconoclastic than I would have liked. I would have preferred to praise the work of Julie Suk, Jo McDougall, Linda Pastan, Philip Levine, Miller Williams, Donald Hall, Sue Ellen Thompson, David Wagoner, Donald Justice, Galway Kinnell, Ernest Sandeen, and W.S. Merwin. The best poems of these writers do what poetry should do. They change our perspective, often forever. They do not show any sign of that spiritual anemia that random, jejune talent and lack of restraint encourage. Poems of these latter tendencies change nothing at all and certainly vindicate the line of Auden quoted at the beginning of this essay.

But when one reads a genuine poem there is no "more after this." There is only the *this* of the poem itself. And the *this-ness* of poetry is what will make its own case and create its own indispensability when it reaches the audience that needs it. Why? Because there is no substitute for it, the politics of poetry notwithstanding. Look at the significance that has justly attached itself to the poetry of Seamus Heaney and Derek Walcott, for instance. They both write in our common language, but their orientation and vision enable them to say things that the American imagination seems incapable of saying for itself. I don't know how much of this is due to the fact that both men are in Walcott's phrase, "ex-colonials" (Heaney from Derry in the north of Ireland and Walcott from St. Lucia and Trinidad). Regardless, they address themselves to the deeper themes of our century and of all time, i.e., human freedom, the lingering historical effects of injustice, the inevitability of suffering, the need of regeneration and the grace of levity from time to time. I suppose that similar sentiments could be made about the work of Czeslaw Milosz or even Borges, but then we might be tempted to wonder why foreign writers seem to possess a poetic maturity that we as Americans too often lack. The poets of anemia lack it absolutely. They seem unaware that poetry is, in the language of Spanish poet Gabriel Celaya, a "weapon loaded with the future." Perhaps the best way to end this essay is to quote Robert Mezey's remarkable translation of Celaya's manifesto to indicate once and for all the vital difference between the poetry of anemia and the poetry that is as necessary to us as oxygen.

When one finally gives up all hope of personal exaltation,
but goes on anyway, quivering, just this side of awareness,
existing savagely, blindly contending,
like a pulse that strikes the darkness,

when the vertiginous
clear eyes of death are seen, face to face,
true things are said:
barbarous, terrible things, tender cruelties—

poems that breathe the spirit
into the starved lungs of so many men, men
who seek life, and music,
who seek some order to the things they feel too deeply.

With the speed of instinct,
with the luminous force of prodigy,
with magical evidence, the real
changes into something identical to itself.

Poetry for the poor, poetry as necessary
as our daily bread,
as the air that we require some thirteen times a minute,
for life, and while we're alive, for saying so with honor.

Because we live by blows, because they leave us
scarcely enough breath to say that we are who we are,
our singing can't just be an ornament and not a crime.
We are touching bottom.

I curse that poetry conceived as a cultural
    luxury for neutrals
who, washing their hands, pretend not to understand and slip away.
I curse the poetry of all who won't take sides till the knife's
    at their throat.

I make these failings my own. I feel so many people
suffering in me, and I sing by drawing breath.
I sing and sing, and singing out beyond my personal
suffering, I am multiplied.

I want to give you life, to incite new acts,
and I count on this with whatever art I have.
I think of myself as an engineer of verse, a worker
like others, who works on Spain, on her steel.

Such is my poetry: ironwork-poetry,
at the same time the heartbeat of something unanimous and
    blind.
That's what it is, a weapon loaded with expanding future,
and I am leveling it at your heart.

It is not a poetry thought out bit by bit.
It is not a perfect product, not a perfect fruit.
It is something like the air we breathe
and the music of space we carry deep inside.

Words which we all repeat, thinking
they're our own, and they vanish. They are more than talk.
They are what is needed most: what has no name.
They are cries out to heaven and, on earth, they are acts.

7

So True as to Be Invisible

Translation occurs when something is changed or transformed into something else, when one thing becomes another. Defined and understood in this way, the very acts of speaking and writing in and of themselves can be regarded as acts of translation—the transformations of feelings or thoughts into sounds or markings that, by common agreement and necessity, stand for those feelings and thoughts—thus making the sharing of experience possible through what is then called communication—or, in the hands of poets, communion. Perhaps life itself can be seen as an act of translation or a series of acts of translation from conception into fetus, fetus into infant, infant into child, child into adolescent, adolescent into adult—a sequence of changes or transformations beginning with the infinitesimal, which contains, in potency, everything that follows it, and continuing to the final stages of life. And for those who believe in the immortality of the soul, death itself can be regarded as an act of translation in which life, in the language of one of the major liturgies, is changed but not taken away—simply translated.

   The art of literary translation is but one subdivision of transla-
tion considered in more cosmic terms. But it differs from most
other translations in that it has about it the aura of absurdity. Why?
Because it is predicated upon impossibility, and indeed it comes into
existence in the face of impossibility. How, some people ask, can the
depth of feeling and the unique vision expressed in one language be
rendered faithfully in another? Isn't the very attempt, they argue, a
desecration of the original? The purists of this world would support
such a position, and in one sense they are nothing but right. But
their very absolutism, if carried to its logical conclusion, would do
nothing but incarcerate us within the prison of our own language,
leading us back to being citizens of the ground-floor of Babel (a
convenient synonym for the face of the earth) where no one would
understand or try to understand the literature of anybody outside of
his own linguistic tribe. On the other hand, those who give a spiritual
and not simply a literal meaning to brotherhood and universality
and internationality would not be so exclusionist. They would say
that the translator—absurdity and impossibility notwithstand-
ing—attempts to create understanding where none was or is thought
possible. This is especially true where poetry is concerned. If T.S.
Eliot was correct when he said that poetry communicates before it
is understood—and I for one think that he was—and I would add
that remains true even when we are listening to poetry in a tongue
that we ourselves do not comprehend—, then the translator aids us
immeasurably by helping us understand what we are feeling by giving
us a bridge of words between the opposing shores of two languages.
Without translators attempting the impossible, what would be the
consequences? I will not further elaborate on the metaphor of Babel,
although the temptation is almost irresistible. I will simply say that
we would of necessity be limited to our native literatures. Americans
would know their Whitman, their Eliot, their cummings, their Hart
Crane, their Robert Frost, their Randall Jarrell and their Richard
Wilbur, but they would not know Dante Alighieri, Pushkin, Goethe,
Cervantes, the troubadours, Sophocles, the great Hebrew poets of
Spain, the pre-Islamic Arabic poets, the poets of China and Japan

and, finally, the Bible. Yet all these are ours for the reading because translators have dared them into English or Anglo-American, have attempted to approximate the originals so that even the translated work becomes an original in its own right, have tried to make their translations so true as to be invisible in order that the spirit of the poet, in whatever tongue, comes through. John Berger came close to saying the same thing when he wrote: "Every poem that works as a poem is an original. And original has two meanings; it means a return to the origin, the first which engendered everything that followed, and it means that which has never occurred before. In poetry, and in poetry alone, the two senses are mated in such a way that they are no longer contradictory."

Let me continue by describing the ideal translator as one who is fluent—spiritually as well as linguistically—in the language from which he is translating and equally fluent—spiritually as well as linguistically—in the language into which he is transposing the original. This is a high qualification, and most translators do not and cannot meet it. Indeed even the possession of such spiritual and linguistic fluency in the ideal translator I have described is of dubious value if the translator is not of the same visionary orientation as the person he is translating. Translating a vision is more than translating words, just as performing Mozart or Chopin is more than playing notes. It is somehow translating the untranslatable. How this is done remains a mystery even to the translator himself. A good translator, for example, may do justice to one author and fail utterly with another in much the same way in which a person may flourish by working in one geographical area and not grow at all if he moves to another even though he may be doing the same work in both. The mystery of success in translation is just that—a mystery. It is a combination of talent, persistence, inspiration, insight, empathy and not a little luck.

And there are pitfalls. Some translators, for instance, have been faulted because they used a poem by a poet they have translated as the occasion for creating their own poem—indebted, obliquely, to the original but essentially the translator's poem. Robert Lowell was charged with this indulgence in a book he frankly entitled *Imitations*. For my part I don't know exactly how this can be avoided. After all, the translator does re-create the poem he is translating from another language into his own through the prism of his own personality, and some of that personality is bound to find its way into the translation. In some cases it may be pure egotism. In other cases it may result in a poem that is poetically inferior to the original. Or the reverse. I have been told that Omar Khayyam is regarded as a third or fourth-rate poet in Persian, but Edward Fitzgerald made Khayyam's "Rubaiyat" sing in his English quatrains. Would it have been better to have a fourth-rate translation of a fourth-rate piece of work or to have done, as Fitzgerald did, a first-rate work that the original spawned but was still indubitably Fitzgerald's? Would anyone hearing Fitzgerald's lines want them any different?

> As much as Wine has play'd the Infidel,
> And robb'd me of my Robe of Honour—well,
> > I often wonder what the Vinters buy
> One half so precious as the Goods they sell.

> Alas, that Spring should vanish with the Rose!
> That Youth's sweet-scented Manuscript should close!
> > The Nightingale that in the Branches sang,
> Ah, whence, and whither flown again, who knows!

> Ah, love! could thou and I with Fate conspire
> To grasp this sorry Scheme of Things entire,
> > Would we not shatter it to bits—and then
> Re-mould it nearer to the Heart's Desire!

A good translator has been called a kind of mid-wife, but I prefer a different analogy. Let us for the sake of amusement—if not for clarity—compare him to a cook. A cook takes things from their natural environment—vegetables from the ground, fruit from the tree, fish from the water, meat from livestock on the hoof—and translates them into ingredients for cooking. As long as they remain in their uncooked condition, they remain ingredients—as literal translations remain literal translations before they are mysteriously transformed into good translations. Then through his imagination and the mystery of fire and herbs and spices and sauces, the cook converts these ingredients into something we can eat and indeed want to eat—into food. A bad translation—to continue the analogy—is like a bad meal. We wish we had not eaten it, but we come to this conclusion only after we have eaten it. Here, for instance, is Clinton Bailey's translation of a poem by a Bedouin named Anez abu Salim about Anwar Sadat's visit to Jerusalem—a poem commissioned by the head of Egypt's Socialist Union Party.

> The will for peace which made Sadat embark on such a mission
> Brought those who ruled along with him to take up his position.
> Each speech they gave was followed by a din of ululation;
> Those who held the reins received the people's adulation.
>
> If someone were a traitor, he would act in ways unknown,
> And betray the Arabs' lands and borders while he gained his own.
> Families lose their homes in war, and many men are slain;
> The losers number many more than those that maybe gain.
> Anwar is choice, a leader, a healer, a saint,
> And for his pains we owe him our thanks without restraint.

On the other hand when the translation is as good as inspiration and human ability can make it, we quite literally can't get enough of it. I find this true time and time again when I read the translations of Edmund Keeley from Greek. Whether he is translating George Seferis, Yannis Ritsos or any contemporary Greek poet, I have rarely found a translation that did not work well—sometimes hauntingly well—in English. Perhaps this is because Mr. Keeley comes as close as anyone to fulfilling my definition of the ideal translator. He has lived in Greece, is fluent in Greek and knew personally most if not all of the poets whose work he translated. Add to this that he is a genuine scholar of contemporary Greek literature, that he is a creative writer himself as well as a critic, and finally that he is fluent and literally sensitive in English. The result is often a masterpiece of translation as with "Mathios Pascalis Among the Roses" by George Seferis:

> I have been smoking since morning without break
> if I stop the roses will embrace me
> with thorns and with fallen petals they will choke me
> they all grow crookedly with the same rose color
> they are staring; they are waiting to see someone; no one passes;
> behind the smoke of my pipe I watch them
> on a weary stalk without fragrance,
> in the other life a woman would say to me you may touch this hand
> and this rose is yours it is yours you may take it
> now or later, whenever you wish.
>
> I descend ever smoking, the stairs
> the roses descend with me in excitement
> and there is something in their manner of the voice
> at the root of shrieking at the point where man
> begins to cry out "mother" or "help me"
> or the small white cries of love.
>
> It is a small garden full of rose bushes
> a few square yards that sink with me
> as I descend the stairs, skyless;
> and her aunt would say to her, "Antigone, you forgot to do
>   your exercises today
> at your age I never wore a corset, not in my time."
> Her aunt was a pitiful creature with protruding veins
> she had many wrinkles about her ears and a moribund nose
> but her words were full of prudence always.
> One day I caught her touching Antigone's breasts
> like a small child stealing an apple.

Will I meet the old woman perhaps as I am descending?
She said to me when I left, "Who knows when we shall meet again?"

Later I read of her death in some old newspapers
of Antigone's wedding and the wedding of Antigone's daughter
with no end to the stairs nor to my tobacco
that imparts to me the taste of a haunted ship
with a mermaid crucified, while she was still beautiful, on the wheel.

A good translator is quite literally a gift to an author. He can be the difference between international attention and oblivion. Jerzy Kosinski, whose novels were translated into a multiplicity of languages, told me that he tried to meet each of his translators—so sensitive was he to the importance of the translator in the distribution of his work abroad. And the Russian poet Andre Voznesensky became well-known in the United States primarily as a result of having his work translated by excellent poets who were determined to do right by him in English because they felt attuned to his style: William Jay Smith, Stanley Kunitz, Richard Wilbur, to name but a few. Having mentioned Wilbur, I cannot refrain from adding that his translations have made the plays of Molière playable. The director and actress Zoe Caldwell once emphasized this to me. She said that she was hired to direct *Tartuffe* in which a translation other than Wilbur's was scheduled for use. Both she and the actors found the translation virtually unactable. It was at this point that she insisted on the Wilbur translation as the only one she was content to use, and the play proceeded thereafter from rehearsal to production without a hitch. And all because Molière was the beneficiary of a brother-soul who chose to be his translator. From this point let me be personal and speak about my own attempts at translation from French and Arabic (plus one poem from Russian): how I proceeded, what I learned, what I am still learning. My first attempt was a translation from French of the lyrical essays on mythology by the distinguished Swiss author and federalist Denis de Rougemont. I worked with a linguist since my own French was plodding at best. Indeed one of the results was a coincidence between my translation and history that remains for me to this day a miracle. In one of the essays in this book de Rougemont includes a line that describes the undertones that exist beneath what we call reality, beneath appearances—the archetypal or mythological truths that manifest themselves from time to time in the world—how heroism comes to light through the actions of specific heroes, how the ideal of feminine beauty is variously revealed through the beauty of specific women, and so forth; de Rougemont called this undertone (literally) "The flow of deeper waters." I liked the literal translation, but I changed the rather flat word "flow" to "growl" in the published text. Simultaneously I was trying to explain to de Rougemont that the book's title in French, *Doctrine Fabuleuse,* did not and could not convey in English (*Fabulous Doctrine*) the connotations of *fable* as he understood the word—that "fabulous" in English meant something so vacuous (as in "fabulous trip" or "fabulous job") that it meant almost nothing at all. He told me to feel free to come up with another title, and I began toying with the idea of calling the book *The Growl of Deeper Waters.* And the book was published subsequently under that title. In the late 1980's Robert McGuire published under the imprint of the Princeton University Press a history of the Bollingen Series—a series funded by Paul Mellon which will always be one of the most distinguished publishing ventures in the history of American publishing. McGuire noted that one of the earliest publications was a book by Denis de Rougemont called *The Devil's Share.* De Rougemont subsequently came to New York, working with various resistance groups against the Nazis. McGuire noted further that de Rougemont had envisioned and committed himself to writing a book about mythology. The working title he chose at the time was *The Growl of Deeper Waters.* I was—to put it mildly—startled out of my wits. I telephoned McGuire and told him about this phenomenal coincidence—how a book that was simply a possibility in the mind of the author in the 1940's would eventually be published in French with the title *Doctrine Fabuleuse,* then be translated and entitled with the very title—to the very word—that was in the author's mind thirty plus years earlier. We were dumbfounded, and we remain so to this day.

The next venture I made as a translator was to turn a selection of poems by the Damascene poet Adonis (Ali Ahmed Said) into English. Again I worked with a linguist but with trepidation since Arabic at its poetic best tends to be an imagistic and aphoristic language. I had tried my hand earlier by translating the work of two other Arabic poets, and the results were ludicrous. What was picturesque and mellifluent in Arabic became sentimental and almost Swinburnian in English. I took some consolation from the fact that my failures were at least noble.

But with Adonis—and this was true before as well as after I met him—I felt I was with someone whose vision and way of thinking or feeling or felt-thinking were akin to my own. When I attempted to translate his poems, the spirit of his poetry seemed almost to glide into English, as in the following poem entitled "The Days":

> My eyes are tired, tired of days,
> tired regardless of days.
> Still must I drill
> through wall after wall
> of days to find another day?
> Is there, is there another day?

The more I worked on Adonis' poems, the more I discovered that the Arabic imagination does things to English that the western imagination seems incapable of doing. Take, for example, these two words (literally translated) that describe the cramped and frenzied fluttering of a butterfly that is held captive within a cage of cupped fingers of two hands—"jailed astonishment." How evocative, how daring, how simply different, and, finally how perfect.

My work with Adonis led to a few other translations that I did for Selma Jayussi in her Columbia University Press volume, *Modern Arabic Poetry.* The results were mixed.

   The next major effort I made in translation was a sequence of poems by Nadia Tueni called *Lebanon: Twenty Poems for One Love*. These were poems written by Mrs. Tueni in French (but, as I was told recently by a close friend of hers, in French words that were linguistically close to their Arabic counterparts) as a kind of poetic geography or map of Lebanon despite its gradual disintegration and destruction by feuding internal parties and the Israeli invasion. It is a testament not only of memory but of history itself. She lists twenty separate and uniquely Lebanese subjects or keystones: individual cities, towns and villages, the famous cedars of Lebanon, the women and men of the mountains and so forth. After I worked over the versions that I made from the transliterations, I arranged to go over the poems (Mrs. Tueni died in 1983) with her husband, Ghassan Tueni, the prominent editor, publisher, author and former ambassador of Lebanon to the United States. He is a man who is absolutely devoted to his wife's memory and her poetry, and his wish to have a good version of the Lebanon poems in English (they already had been translated into Arabic) was just as intense as my own. I thought and still think the poems beautiful, but Ambassador Tueni's taste in poetry was more Tennysonian than mine, and we had a good many disagreements about how the poems would work best in English. Some of them were minor. Should it be "Byblos, my beloved" or "My beloved Byblos." Some involved a knowledge of background—there is a small village where, as a native Lebanese knew, the inhabitants kept basil plants in their flower boxes so that the whole village smelled of basil. This explained one of the images in one of the poems. The result of all this backing-and-forthing was uniquely satisfying to me, and in retrospect all the efforts were well worth it.

IN THE LEBANESE MOUNTAINS

Remember—the noise of moonlight
when the summer night collides with a peak
and traps the wind
in the rocky caves of the mountains of Lebanon.

Remember—a town on a sheer cliff
set like a tear on the rim of an eyelid;
one discovers there a pomegranate tree
and rivers more sonorous than a piano.

Remember—the grapevine under the fig tree,
the cracked oak that September waters,
fountains and muleteers,
the sun dissolving in the river currents.

Remember—the basil and apple tree,
mulberry syrup and almond groves.
Each girl was a swallow then
whose eyes moved like a gondola
swung from a hazel branch.

Remember—the hermit and goatherd,
paths that rise to the edge of a cloud,
the chant of Islam, crusaders' castles,
and wild bells ringing through July.

Remember—each one, everyone,
storyteller, prophet and baker,
the words of the feast and the words of the storm,
the sea shining like a medal in the landscape.

Remember—the child's recollection
of a secret kingdom just our age.
We did not know how to read the omens
in those dead birds in the bottoms of their cages,
in the mountains of Lebanon.

WOMEN OF MY COUNTRY

Women of my country,
a common light hardens your bodies,
and a common darkness lets them rest
in a soft elegy of change.
A common suffering cracks your lips,
and your eyes have been set by the same unique jeweler.
You reassure mountains,
convince ashes of their own fertility
and tell the land that it will never pass away.
Women of my country,
even in chaos you discover what endures.

8

One Definite Mozart

Ever since I first began reading Richard Wilbur's poems in the late 1940's, I think I've read only one negative review of his work. It was not Randall Jarrell's somewhat patronizing critique of Wilbur's second book, *Ceremony*, but a review of *The Mind-Reader* by Calvin Bedient in *The New Republic* (June 5, 1976). Bedient contended that Wilbur was too safe a poet—that he rarely took chances. Bedient was not referring to subject matter; he was taking Wilbur to task for his deliberately choosing to remain within the limits of traditional metrics and prosody and yielding to "moral complacency."

I mention this now because one of my themes in this appreciation will be to demonstrate that Richard Wilbur's refreshing and refreshened traditionalisms along the lines of metrics and prosody are not a weakness but a strength and that "moral complacency" has nothing to do with that. And I make this statement as one not fully enthralled by that tradition as it is literally defined but fully supportive of Wilbur's achievements within it. To say smugly that Wilbur never took chances is to betray a superficial reading of Wilbur's work to date. The nuances of diversity and experiment are everywhere, and they serve to re-create rather than merely perpetuate the set patterns of quatrains, couplets, sonnets, pentameters, trimeters, or even the alliteratively linked linear segments that Wilbur adapted from the Anglo-Saxon scops. That he has done so with almost Elizabethan elegance is what has distinguished his poetry among that of all his contemporaries from the time of the publication of *The Beautiful Changes* in 1947 to the appearance of *New and Collected Poems* in 1988, for which he received his second Pulitzer Prize, and finally to the most recent *Mayflies* in 2000 and a second collected edition in 2004. That he has been criticized by some who lack his consistent virtuosity within the chosen disciplines that he has embraced and with which he feels most comfortable is perhaps inevitable. But to me this is not unlike criticizing a tennis player for playing tennis (also an activity governed by fixed rules) exceptionally well on, of all things, a tennis court. Even if one does not like the game or the rules, one can at least respect the talent of one who has mastered them, re-created them in his own style and advanced and enriched the tradition by performing well within its strictures.

On the other hand, Calvin Bedient may simply not have been impressed by how a poem by Wilbur reads—how it evolves from the first word to the last. Those who believe that poetry is a mere stream of consciousness or that the language of poetry is nothing but the language of accidental associative meanings or that poetry is a kind of imaginative ink blot whose destiny is simply to expand itself to the limits of exhaustion will assuredly not read Richard Wilbur with pleasure. His work does not accommodate such frivolity. As a poet he has definite syllogistic way of thinking; his poems have a beginning, middle and an end that parallel the way we think from assertion to judgment. Not all of them follow the "If …but …therefore" mode of syllogistic logic, but a good many of them do, and the imprint of this way of thinking is characteristic of a mind that does not meander but concludes. Shakespeare's sonnets impress us with a similar way of thinking, which further accentuates my inclination to call Wilbur's style Elizabethan. Wilbur's poems seem to obey an inner imperative that is intellectual rather than emotional, or perhaps I should say emotionally intellectual. We sense that the poet is actually thinking through his feelings to their inevitable and ineluctable conclusion.

So much for preface and apologia. It is not my intent to defend Richard Wilbur against mere carping but to appreciate and admire his poetry that consistently rewards every moment of attention devoted to it. Rather than concentrate on Wilbur's evident technical virtuosity, I propose to focus on his artistic restraint, his genuine mirth, his sense of the tragic and his overall—for lack of a better word—felicity. By felicity I mean language that is happy with itself in the contexts that this poet has created for it. As a rule Wilbur is such a felicitous poet except in those rare instances when he seems to be willing a poem into existence because something has aroused his indignation before his inspiration and talent can fully digest it.

To call Wilbur a formalist, as he has been called by many throughout his career, is simply to acknowledge that he writes within the established traditions of English and American poetics. But formalism is too pat a label to paste on any poet, and it clarifies little. The same could be said of Anthony Hecht or Stanley Kunitz, but so what? Isn't it more helpful to speak of Wilbur's restraint within his chosen formalisms, his peculiar aesthetic reserve that eschews the "let-it-all-hang-out" approach in favor of choosing the most miniscule detail that is capable of being the key to everything? For example, he does not flail blindly at the barbarism of war (which, as in infantryman in World War II, he must have seen at close quarters) but concentrates on a lonely sentry in "First Snow in Alsace" who is momentarily distracted by snow-swirls and snow-designs so that he ignores the whitening shell-holes, the snowdrifts on the ammunition stacks and, stunningly, the "snowfall (that) fills the eyes/Of soldiers dead a little while." Nor in another poem called "Place Pigalle" does he moralize about the whores and stripshows but somehow intermingles the lust and loneliness of soldiers on leave from the front who search out "their ancient friends" with the poignancy of a midsummer night's dream-like respite from a war that makes murderers out of young men who might otherwise be lovers:

> Ionized innocence: this pair reclines,
> She on the table, he in a tilting chair,
> With Arden ease; her eyes as pale as air
> Travel his priestgoat face; his hand's thick tines
> Touch the gold whorls of her Corinthian hair.
>
> "Girl, if I love thee not, then let me die;
> Do I not scorn to change my state with kings?
> Your muchtouched flesh, incalculable, which wrings
> Me so, now shall I gently seize in my
> Desperate soldier's hands, which kill all things."

This poem illustrates Wilbur's restraint at its finest. The result is that the theme is strengthened by what is held back. I do not find this to be the case with "On the Eyes of an SS Officer," which ends with this explicit final stanza:

> But this one's iced or ashen eyes devise,
> Foul purities, in flesh their wilderness,
> Their fire; I ask my makeshift God of this
> My opulent bric-a-brac earth to damn his eyes.

The rhetoric of hatred is here, but the directness of its expression makes the poetry evaporate for me. Wilbur does not suffer such lapses often, but they do occur. Perhaps this is because his basic optimistic and open nature does not easily transmute rage and indignation into the stuff of poetry. Dante, of course, could do it. Neruda did it when his inspiration and indignation fused; otherwise he simply versified a lot of personal bile and propaganda. Wilbur is capable of the right indignations, which means that he is outraged at the right times, but his moral umbrage often strips him of the restraint that is the fertile growing ground of his poetic talent. The difference is immediately noticeable in the aforementioned poem as well as in the concluding sestet of his "A Miltonic Sonnet for Mr. Johnson on His Refusal of Peter Hurd's Official Portrait."

> Rightly you say the picture is too large
> Which Peter Hurd by your appointment drew,
> And justly call that Capitol too bright
> Which signifies our people in your charge;
> Wait, Sir, and see how time will render you
> Who talk of vision but are weak of sight.

I suppose a case could be made for this poem as a re-creation of the Miltonic spirit in our time, but Wilbur's language has too direct an indebtedness to Milton for me to see it as anything more than an adaptation, despite the contemporaneity of the subject matter. The fact remains that Wilbur's formidable talent does not appear at its best when he is moved to write like this. It is not that one disagrees with his moral or political positions (agreement or disagreement is not relevant here) but with the way they are stated or rendered. Having known him more than casually for several decades, I would say that certain social or political issues affect him deeply and that he sincerely would like to take issue with guile or chicanery or plain wrongdoing through a poetic vision rather than through speeches, letters and the like. But such poems fail as poems more often than they succeed, despite Wilbur's efforts to place them in the tradition of righteous anger, as with the just quoted Miltonic sonnet. Take his "Speech for the Repeal of the McCarren Act" as another example. Wilbur invokes Mercian figures as the basis for his central metaphor, but his rhetorical impulses still get the better of his poetic ones. In short, the style of his utterance in this hectoring vein seems to be adapted, not natural. And I attribute this to temperament. Some poets can make poems out of spleen so that their poetry seems a logical extension of their talent. But Wilbur's poems in this genre seem muscled into being; they lose in similitude what they gain in directness, and poetry is in the former more than in the latter. I will rest my case by quoting a few lines as evidence from a poem Wilbur wrote in 1970 entitled "For the Student Strikers."

> Go talk with those who are rumored to be unlike you,
> And whom, it is said, you are so unlike.
> Stand on the stoops of their houses and tell them why
> You are out on strike.
>
> It is not yet time for the rock, the bullet, the blunt
> Slogan that fuddles the mind toward force.
> Let the new sound in our street be the patient sound
> Of your discourse.

Having expressed what is probably my only reservation about Wilbur's talent, I now feel free to praise. And I have no intention of being stingy in my praise of a man who, in poetic terms, is possibly the Mozart of our time. What Mozart achieved in music has a counterpart in Wilbur's achievement in poetry, particularly in his sense of symmetry, his uncanny precision of word choice, his almost infallible ear, his sense of humor as well as his sense of the tragic within a historical and literary tradition that he knows only too well, and, finally, his basic Christian ethos and the worldview that it nurtures.

To speak of Wilbur's sense of symmetry means more than the appearance of the poem on the page, although even from that perspective the basic layout of a Wilbur poem gives one an immediate impression of entirety—an impression that a subsequent reading of the poem immediately confirms. His poems end in conclusions, not confusions. The conclusions may flow from an idea advanced early in the poem, or, as in "Piazza de Spagna, Early Morning," the elaboration of a single image:

I can't forget
How she stood at the top of that long marble stair
     Amazed, and then with a sleepy pirouette
Went dancing slowly down to the fountain-quieted square.

     Nothing upon her face
But some impersonal loneliness,—not then a girl,
     But as it were a reverie of the place,
     A called-for failing glide and whirl;

     As when a leaf, petal, or thin chip
Is drawn to the falls of a pool and circling a moment above it,
     Rides on over the lip—
     Perfectly beautiful, perfectly ignorant of it.

He does something quite similar in "A Glance from the Bridge."

Letting the eyes descend from reeking stack
And black façade to where the river goes,
You see the freeze has started in to crack
(As if the city squeezed it in a vise),
And here and there the limbering water shows,
And gulls colonial on the sullied ice.

Some rise and braid their glidings white and spare,
Or sweep the hemmed-in river up and down,
Making a litheness in the barriered air,
And through the town the freshening water swirls
As if an ancient whore undid her gown
And showed a body almost like a girl's.

The most regular poetic progressions in Wilbur's work appear in the riddle poems or what's-my-name poems that have been part of his writing from the very beginning (they spilled over delightfully into a book called *Opposites* whose meters challenge and whose rhymes please both children and adults.)These poems are not mere puzzles to be solved; they have about them a wit and whimsy that keeps them enjoyable even after the solution is known. The poetry is in their very structure and resolution with each poem ending, as Yeats once said of good poems in general, like the lid of a jewelry box being snapped shut. Here, for example, is one of the riddles of Symphosius—a three-liner describing coinage:

> First I was earth and deep in earth retired;
> Another name I gained when I was fired;
> I'm earth no more, but through me earth's acquired.

Another example of Wilbur's sense of symmetry, though somewhat atypical, is the following single image entitled "Sleepless at Crown Point":

> All night, this headland
> Lunges into the rumpling
> Capework of the wind.

This symmetry in Wilbur's best poems is never imposed. It seems to proceed from the poetic seed out of which each poem grows, and Wilbur is artist enough (negatively capable enough, to use Keats' phrase) to go with the flow of this poetic energy until the poem has completed itself. If his poems were chairs or tables, I would always be convinced that their sutures and fastenings were secure and that they could stand on their own. At least, this has been my experience. I know from my reading of his work for more than forty years that he has never permitted himself to release something for publication that is not complete. At a time when some of his contemporaries regard opaqueness as a virtue rather than a sign of immaturity, this is no small triumph. And, of course, Wilbur's ongoing concern with the exact meaning and connotation and sound of words is a further aspect of his talent that places him in direct (and, for me, happy) opposition to some modern poets described as by C. M. Cioran in his *Anathemas and Admirations* as follows:

> Poetry *is threatened* when poets take too lively a theoretical interest in language and make it into a constant subject of meditation, when they confer upon it an exceptional status.... If we are truly to think, thought must adhere to the mind; if it becomes independent of the mind, exterior to it, the mind is shackled from the start, idles, and has but one source left—itself—instead of relying on the world for its substance or its pretexts. The writer must guard against reflecting obsessively upon language, must avoid making it the subject of his obsessions, must never forget that the important works have been created *despite* language. Dante was obsessed with what he had to say, not by the saying of it.

I do not think it presumptuous to claim that these words might have been written by Wilbur himself since his concern has always been with the things of this world and how to re-create them in language; in any case, I doubt if he would take exception to them. He is concerned with language the way that a landscape painter is concerned with paint. He constantly searches for the right word as a painter might search for the right (the exactly right) color to express his vision. He identifies the song of bells, for example, as the "the selfsame toothless voice for death or bridal." He alludes at just the right moment in "The Melongene" to the purple presence of an eggplant and, presto, we are in the eggplant's presence. In "Potato" he is able to distinguish the pure potato smell: "Cut open raw," in two lines: the essence of it "looses a cool clean stench,/Mineral acid seeping from pores of priest meal." His poetic obituary to Phelps Putnam ("To an American Poet Just Dead") contains the "ssshh of sprays on all the little lakes" and an allusion to immortality as a "higher standard of living." In "Driftwood" he writes of "the great generality of waters" and the "warped" pieces having the look of

"excellence earned" by retaining "their dense/ingenerate grain. " In
"An Event" he perceives in the zigzag of clouds of birds in flight
"By what cross-purposes the world is dreamt." And "A Baroque
Wall-Fountain in the Villa Sciara" contains one of the best re-cre-
ations of the sound and sight of fountaining water that I have ever
encountered in any literature:

> Happy in all that ragged, loose
> Collapse of water, its effortless descent
>
> And flatteries of spray,
> The stocky god upholds the shell with ease,
> Watching, about his craggy knees,
> The goatish innocence of his babes at play;
>
> His fauness all the while
> Leans forward, slightly, into the clambering mesh
> Of water-lights, her sparkling flesh
> In a saecular ecstasy, her blinded smile
>
> Bent on the sand floor
> Of the trefoil pool, where ripple-shadows come
> And go in swift reticulum,
> More addling to the eye than wine, and more
>
> Interminable to thought
> Than pleasure's calculus. Yet since this all
> Is pleasure, flash, and waterfall,
> Must it not be too simple? Are we not
>
> More intricately expressed
> In the plain fountains that Maderna set
> Before St. Peter's—the main jet
> Struggling aloft until it seems to rest

> In the very act of rising, until
> The very wish of water is reversed,
>   That heaviness borne up to burst
> In a clear high, cavorting head, to fill
>
>   With blaze, and then in gauze
> Delays, in a gnatlike shimmering, in a fine
>   Illumined version of itself, decline
> And patter on the stones its own applause?

It is in stanzas like these that one can detect how Wilbur's ear rarely fails him. The matching of sound and rhythm to the rise and fall of fountaining water is so unobtrusively true that we actually hear as well as see the "wish of water" in and through the language. I for one admire the subtlety here of Wilbur's musical sense more than I do some of the onomatopoetic stanzas of "On Freedom's Ground"(Part IV) where he attempts to replicate the rhythms of waltzes, polkas, cakewalks, and jigs. Of course, these replications occur in a cantata where the words cannot be divorced from the musical background—they are lyrics, after all—, but I find the silent music of the lines he wrote to evoke the waterflow of the Villa Sciara fountain more poetic.

As he has grown older, Wilbur has not abandoned the formal hallmarks of his earlier style (as Karl Shapiro did, for example) but adapted them to different subjects with the same jeweler's eye and musician's ear for the right world in the right place at exactly the right time. Poems like "The Fire-Truck" and "The Undead" from *Advice to a Prophet* (1961) testify to this as does the book's powerful title poem. Nor does Wilbur's basic style change in *Walking to Sleep* (1969) in such poems as "For Dudley," "Playboy," and "A Late Aubade."

The poem called "Shame" in *Advice to a Prophet* is a happy aberration. True, the lines are basically iambic pentameter lines, but they are certainly not in the tradition of Pope's precise ten-syllabled pentameters. Wilbur hews to five feet per line, but he plays fast and loose with the syllabic count, and the poem is much better for it because the fastness and looseness match the theme. This is one of the few poems in which Wilbur just lets himself go, and his sense of mild sarcasm, his basic good humor and his almost Rabelaisian swagger here and there (usually hidden elsewhere to the point of invisibility) rise and flourish to the plain delight of any fair-minded reader. Anyone familiar with the poem knows how the unspecified country of "Shame" achieves its ultimate victory over its conquerors and occupiers. Wilbur informs us early in the poem that this is a nation with "no foreign policy," an unfathomable grammar, a national sense of its own unimportance, and a geography "best described as unrelieved." The people's chief weapon seems to be self-depreca-tion wedded to self-disdain. Left alone, they turn these weapons on themselves and manage thus to perpetuate their own mediocrity and undisguised mendacity. After all, this is a country whose "national product" is sheep and whose people truly believe that "they do not count" and who confirm this by announcing that the population total is "zero."

   Yet, their very vices make them invincible when they confront the "hoped-for invasion" with "complete negligence" and "overwhelm-ing submission." The result is that they conquer their conquerors by slowly imbuing them with their own vices:

> Their complete negligence is reserved, however,
> For the hoped-for invasion, at which time the happy people
> (Sniggering, ruddily naked, and shamelessly drunk)
> Will stun the foe by their overwhelming submission,
> Corrupt the generals, infiltrate the staff,
> Usurp the throne, proclaim themselves to be sun-gods
> And bring about the collapse of the whole empire.

Further confirming Wilbur's sense of artistic restraint during the sixties are two touchstone poems—one from *Advice to a Prophet* and the other from *Walking to Sleep*. The title poem from *Advice to a Prophet* is not a direct but a slantwise comment on the possibility of a nuclear apocalypse, though Wilbur eschews the apocalyptic tone and pose so readily assumed by numerous other poets dealing with the same subject. He asks not to be informed about "the weapons, their force and range," nor does he want to be told for the zillionth time about the possible extinction of humanity ("Nor shall you scare us with talk of the death of the race"). Instead Wilbur considers the realizable desolation we would immediately know if certain specific animals or birds were to disappear from the earth as we know it. He does not speak in general or abstract terms of the death of mankind but of finite, definite absences, and the sense of loss that is at the heart of the poem grows out of these anticipated absences:

> ...Though we cannot conceive
> Of an undreamt thing, we know to our cost
> How the dreamt cloud crumbles, the vines are blackened
>   by frost,
> How the view alters. We could believe
>
> If you told us so, that the white-tailed deer will slip
> Into perfect shade, grown perfectly shy,
> The lark avoid the reaches of our eye,
> The jack-pine lose its knuckled grip
>
> On the cold ledge, and every torrent burn
> As Xanthus, once, its gliding trout
> Stunned in a twinkling. What should we be without
> The dolphin's arc, the dove's return
>
> These things in which we have seen ourselves and
>   spoken?
> Ask us, prophet, how we shall call
> Our natures forth when that live tongue is all
> Dispelled, that glass obscured or broken

In which we have said the rose of our love and the
     clean
Horse of our courage, in which beheld
The singing locust of the soul unshelled,
And all we mean, or wish to mean.

The power of this poem derives from how we respond to those prophesied and enumerated losses and the effect their absence will have on how we define our very lives. The extent of this loss is left to our imaginations. In terror as in art, less proves to be more, much more.

    The poem "Running" from *Walking to Sleep* is structurally a typical Wilbur poem—a series of introductory descriptions in each section with each ambience counterbalanced by the poet's reaction to it. All three sections deal straightforwardly with the joyful exhilaration of running or of observing runners in action. In the first section Wilbur remembers running in Caldwell, New Jersey, in 1933. The lickety-split run becomes an absolute in his memory when he writes—"Thinking of happiness, I think of that." Skipping the second section for a moment, we find in the third section a self-description where Wilbur running as an older man comes upon two boys running in the opposite direction. As they prepare to pass one another, they rhyme for a moment simply as runners, and Wilbur senses the exhilaration of youth from that passing moment. But it is in the second section that we find the correlative that is possibly an inadvertent profile that Wilbur gives of himself. Wilbur, now a non-participant, focuses on one of the runners in a race:

Dark in the glare, they seemed to thresh in place
Like preening flies upon a window-sill,
Yet gained and grew, and at a cruel pace
Swept by us on their way to Heartbreak Hill—

Legs driving, fists at port, clenched faces, men,
And in amongst them, stamping on the sun,

Our champion Kelley, who would win again,
Rocked in his will, at rest within his run.

The style of Kelley's run is a perfect match for Wilbur's style as a writer—a man sure of his skills and strengths, secure within his own skin, husbanding his known resources and then pitting them against nothing but the challenge before him, confident that he is equal to it.

It may not be important to some to identify humor as one of Wilbur's poetic assets, but I for one believe it is. Humor is also a sign of a person with a sense of spiritual balance. Although Robert Lowell was and remains a poet of genuine stature and has been identified as a more cosmic poet than Wilbur, one must look long and hard to find a Lowell poem with a smile on its face. Nonetheless, a sense of humor would have gone a long way to acquaint us with his very humanity and not merely with his personal demons. Wilbur's humor, whether ribald enough to provoke a loud guffaw or subtle enough to coax a good chuckle, is never mean-spirited or silly. Its aim seems to be pure fun whether it has a satirical edge or not. And this is true of his earlier poems ("Superiorities," "Parable," "Museum Piece") as well as of subsequent ones ("Shame," "Matthew VIII, 28ff.," "A Late Aubade," "The Prisoner of Zenda," "To His Skeleton"). The spirit of humor in "Matthew VII, 28ff." is a typical example:

Rabbi, we Gadarenes
Are not ascetics; we are fond of wealth and possessions.
Love, as you call it, we obviate by means
Of the planned release of aggressions.

We have deep faith in prosperity.
Soon, it is hoped, we will reach our full potential.
In the light of the gross product, the practice of charity
Is palpably inessential.

It is true that we go insane;

That for no good reason we are possessed by devils;
That we suffer, despite the amenities which obtain
At all but the lowest levels.

We shall not, however, resign
Our trust in the high-heaped table and the full trough.
If you cannot cure us without destroying our swine,
We had rather you shoved off.

The barely concealed criticism of the smugly rich in this poem
somehow does not get in the way of the roistering, and by the time
we get to the last line we are smiling our way into a good laugh.

To move from Wilbur's humorous poems to such masterpieces as
"Love Calls Us to the Thing of This World," "The Writer," "Cottage
Street, 1953," and a love poem to his wife Charlee in *Mayflies* called
"For C" is to realize that Wilbur is not a man who, like some of the
confessionalists of his generation, eschews the lightsome in order to
be properly glum. Not at all. His is a sensibility which permits him to
respond to and re-create in his poetry the light as well as the weighty,
the smile as well as the frown. And who can deny that a complete
vision of human life does not, after all, include them both?

Now to a consideration of the ethos of Wilbur's talent. That Wilbur
has a theocentric view of life is traceable not only to those poems
of his that have liturgical or theological themes, i.e., "A Christmas
Hymn," "A Wedding Toast," "For Dudley," "John Chrysostom,"
to name but a few of the many, but to a deeper and unmistakable
spirituality that infuses his entire corpus and is unfeignable. Three
poems from his total oeuvre reveal to me the three salient aspects of
his spirituality. The first is a crypto-poem called "The Proof" that
is both a prayer and, in its succinctness, a further variation of the
telegrammic style found in his riddles. The second is "Love Calls
Us to the Things of This World," a poem which, in its acceptance of
the given world and its transfiguration in words, is as consummate
a realization as I know of what the calling of a poet as a seer really

means. And the third is "Cottage Street, 1952" because of all that stands behind the naked judgment of the final line.

The tone of "The Proof' (with tone defined as the author's attitude toward his subject, his audience and himself) is as revealing of Wilbur's sensibility as is the very subject of the poem. From the first word to the last the author reveals himself as a trusting and humble man who is willing to abandon himself to the mercy and generosity of God. It is as if Wilbur has taken the biblical injunction that fear of the Lord is the beginning of wisdom and made it the very soul of the poem. I have detected this same tone in numerous other poems of his (and in some of his translations as well). It is never forced nor fictitious. Somehow one is able to sense when one is the presence of genuine feelings of this nature, and the feelings aroused by "The Proof' impress me in this way.

> Shall I love God for causing me to be?
> I was mere utterance; shall these words love me?
>
> Yet when I caused his work to jar and stammer,
> And one free subject loosened all his grammar,
>
> I love him that he did not in a rage
> Once and forever rule me off the page
>
> But, thinking I might come to please him yet,
> Crossed out *delete* and wrote his patient *stet*.

This poem has the unmistakable resignation and deference of personal prayer. It is this deference that appears again and again in Wilbur's poetry—a deference to things as they are in their God-created or man-created uniqueness, a deference to the beautiful and its changes, a deference to love itself and a willingness to allow it the space it needs to manifest itself and grow.

Perhaps no poem in all of Wilbur's writings affirms his wonder in the presence of God-created or man-created things than his much and deservedly anthologized "Love Calls Us to the Things of This World." Rather than quote the poem in its entirety since it is one of Wilbur's best known works, I will allude only to the basic circumstance of the poem and how Wilbur, presumably the persona of the poem, finds in that circumstance a reason to affirm and bless it.

A sleeper is slowly coming awake. He imagines that the laundry hanging on the clothesline outside his window is a flight of seraphim. This angelic laundry seems to float and dance in the "false dawn" of semi-wakefulness:

> Now they are rising together in calm swells
> Of halcyon feeling, filling whatever they were
> With the deep joy of their impersonal breathing

But such a Platonic view has only a limited lease on the observer's life, and, despite how he wants the illusion to persist in defiance of the upcoming "punctual rape of every blessed day," he knows that the soul must descend "once more in bitter love/To accept the waking body." And, of course, since form and function are destined to exist in consonance, the hanging laundry, which exists finally to be worn, must come down from its "ruddy gallows." It must clothe thieves, lovers and nuns; the world must go on being the world. The pivotal image of the lovers ("Let lovers go fresh and sweet to be undone") provides the ironic balance between the thieves and the nuns, since lovers go dressed only to the point when they must undo their clothes so that they can become lovers in fact—lovemakers. Regardless of the irony, the entire poem ends on the side of life and "the things of this world" where only love can humanize us, not in otherworldly but in this-worldly terms. Like Frost, Wilbur assumes that "earth's the right place for love." Thus the waking body offsets the bitterness of its dream-ending moment of false bliss by quite literally blessing (what is an affirmation, after all, but a blessing?) the real world where theft, loving and devotion are ongoing and co-existent.

"Cottage Street, 1953" is Wilbur at his lyrical and perspicacious best. The setting could not be more plain—a tea on Cottage Street hosted by Edna Ward, Wilbur's mother-in-law. Present are Wilbur himself, his wife, a young Sylvia Plath and her mother. Wilbur admits to having been invited so as to serve as a role model for the despondent Sylvia.

> It is my office to exemplify
> The published poet in his happiness,
> Thus cheering Sylvia, who has wished to die;
> But half-ashamed, and impotent to bless,
>
> I am a stupid life-guard who has found
> Swept to his shallows by the tide, a girl
> Who, far from shore, has been immensely drowned
> And stares through water now with eyes of pearl.

The ongoing "refusal" of Sylvia Plath to do anything but drown is in sharp contrast with the quiet courage of Edna Ward, destined to die a decade and a half later (the poem was obviously written after 1968) but doing so with tearless dignity and speaking of love to and at the very end. Against the example of Edna Ward's graced and graceful death at the age of eighty-eight, Wilbur describes Sylvia Plath as one who in her despair seemed "condemned to live" and whose poetry's "brilliant negative" seemed on balance "free and helpless and unjust." It is the mention of injustice that tells us how Wilbur perceives the lives of these two radically different women—the elder, who is a valiant example of keeping faith with life even *in extremis,* and the younger, who is a victim not so much of life as of her twisted vision of it. Weighing Edna Ward's bravery against the spiritual self-betrayal of Sylvia Plath who, at the time of the writing of this poem had already taken her own life, Wilbur comes down on the side of justice—justice to life itself. This transmutes the poem into a double elegy, and, as elegies tell us more about life when touched with death than they tell us about life itself (since death is actually unknowable), they reveal the human values of the elegist himself. Ultimately Wilbur pities Sylvia Plath; he is edified by Edna Ward.

This brings me full circle in my estimate of Richard Wilbur. (I should add that Wilbur is an equally talented reader of his own poems and translations. Whoever has listened to him before an audience has experienced what Wilbur himself ascribed once to the work of Degas—"Beauty joined to energy.") My few reservations, which I felt obliged to include in the spirit of absolute candor, are but quibbles in the balance. Far exceeding them is the wealth of poems that will be part of our literature as long as it lasts. For that we can only be quick to praise and, above all, be grateful.

About the Author

The author of books of poetry, fiction, essays, and plays, Samuel Hazo is the founder and director of the International Poetry Forum in Pittsburgh, Pennsylvania, where he is also McAnulty Distinguished Professor of English Emeritus at Duquesne University, where he taught for 43 years. His recent books are *The Holy Surprise of Right Now* and *As They Sail* (poetry), *Stills* (fiction), *Feather* and *Mano a Mano* (drama) and *Spying for God* (essays). His translations include Denis de Rougemont's *The Growl of Deeper Waters*, Nadia Tueni's *Lebanon: Twenty Poems for One Love*, and Adonis' *The Pages of Day and Night*. His book of poems, *Just Once: New and Previous Poems*, received the Maurice English Poetry Award in 2003, and a new collection of poems entitled *A Flight to Elsewhere* was published in 2005. He was most recently honored with the Griffin Award for Creative Writing from the University of Notre Dame. A National Book Award finalist, he was chosen the first State Poet of the Commonwealth of Pennsylvania by Governor Robert Casey in 1993, and he served until 2003.